A Possible Cinema:
The Films of Alain Tanner

by
Jim Leach

The Scarecrow Press, Inc.
Metuchen, N.J., and London
1984

Library of Congress Cataloging in Publication Data

Leach, Jim.
  A possible cinema.

    Bibliography: p.
    Includes index.
    1. Tanner, Alain. I. Title.
PN1998.A3T264 1984   791.43'0233'0924   84-10610
ISBN 0-8108-1714-4

Copyright © 1984 by Jim Leach

Manufactured in the United States of America

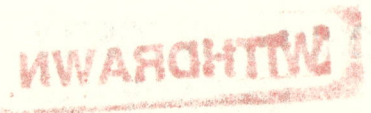

CONTENTS

Illustrations — iv

Preface — v

1. Tanner before Charles — 1
2. Circle and Margin: Tanner in Theory — 27
3. Charles Dead or Alive — 55
4. The Salamander — 71
5. Return from Africa — 90
6. The Middle of the World — 106
7. Jonah Who Will Be 25 in the Year 2000 — 125
8. Messidor — 151
9. Light Years Away — 167
10. Conclusion: Tanner Who Will Be 70 in the Year 2000 — 180

Filmography — 185

Bibliography — 189

Index — 199

ILLUSTRATIONS

Grouped together in special section.

	Page
CHARLES DEAD OR ALIVE	A
THE SALAMANDER	B-C
RETURN FROM AFRICA	C-D
THE MIDDLE OF THE WORLD	D-F
JONAH WHO WILL BE 25 IN THE YEAR 2000	F-H
MESSIDOR	I-J
LIGHT YEARS AWAY	K
IN THE WHITE CITY	L

PREFACE

The achievement of Swiss cinema in the seventies has been widely recognized, and Alain Tanner's films are clearly a major part of that achievement. But the implications of his work extend far beyond the confines of a national cinema. Tanner explores important issues of political and cinematic practice that offer possible alternatives to the ideological stalemate that has developed in the eighties. The "wager" at the core of Tanner's cinema is that it is possible to steer a path between the compromises required by the commercial cinema and the marginal status assigned to a committed political cinema. Although the outcome of this "wager" is still undecided, the aim of this book is to examine its possibilities and to account for the very real pleasure afforded by the films that it has shaped.

The first two chapters attempt to place the films in their cultural and theoretical contexts, but the main concern here is to provide a close analysis of the individual films in order to assess the value of Tanner's overall strategy. In terms of Tanner's own career, this strategy does seem to have become bogged down. His first five films represent a clear progression: Charles Dead or Alive (1969) is a modest co-production with Swiss television; The Salamander (1971) brought Tanner to the attention of wider audiences; Return from Africa (1973) and The Middle of the World (1974) consolidated his position and extended his range; while Jonah Who Will Be 25 in the Year 2000 (1975) was his most ambitious, controversial and successful film to date. However, the two most recent films, Messidor (1979) and Light Years Away (1981), have received only limited distribution and testify to the severe difficulties facing filmmakers who are concerned to create a cinema that is both politically and personally satisfying.

Tanner's future may be problematic, but his films

remain as signposts to a possible cinematic future. Tanner's films, of course, are not the only ones of importance in the movement towards a new cinema, but his strategies and their political implications are significant and need to be taken into account.

1: TANNER BEFORE CHARLES

The appearance of Alain Tanner's Charles Dead or Alive in 1969 was one of the first signs of the emergence of the new Swiss cinema that was to receive widespread acclaim during the seventies. Along with Michel Soutter and Claude Goretta and several other French- and German-speaking filmmakers, Tanner helped to establish a national cinema in a country in which cinematic activity had hitherto been sporadic and largely unsuccessful.[1] The smallness of the country and its linguistic divisions have worked, historically, against the development of a strong Swiss culture, and the economic realities of filmmaking virtually ruled out the possibility of a film industry in such a limited market. Just as Swiss writers and artists tended to be absorbed into the stronger neighboring cultures of which the various Swiss linguistic groups were considered to be extensions, so cinema in Switzerland has been dominated by the industries of the larger countries across the border. In the case of cinema, the problem is heightened by the dominant influence of Hollywood, whose economic power and popular appeal has inhibited the growth of national cinemas throughout the world. By the late sixties, however, the erosion of the studio system in Hollywood and a general decline of confidence in the American dream had weakened Hollywood's economic position to some extent and encouraged the growth of national cinemas that challenged the still-dominant model (notably in Italy and France). Building on these earlier achievements, the Swiss filmmakers were able to take advantage of the new lightweight equipment and television sponsorship to develop their own distinctive approach to cinema.

The critical success of their films came as a surprise, not only because of the size of the ocuntry but because of the image of Switzerland that had developed outside its borders. One of the most notorious of the many sarcastic comments on Swiss culture occurs in <u>The Third Man</u> when Harry Lime compares the flowering of Italian culture under the Borgias with the Swiss situation: "They had brotherly love, five hundred years of democracy and peace, and what did they produce...? The cuckoo clock."[2] The country's reputation for clocks and watches created the image of a society based on precision and regulation, which was accompanied by images from what Tanner has called an "ignoble folklore" centering on chocolate, cheese, and Alpine yodellers.[3] Peace and prosperity were achieved through a policy of neutrality which kept Switzerland out of major European conflicts for centuries, and the combination of security, stability and neutrality has made the country the headquarters of numerous international banks, corporations and government agencies. Despite the early development of democratic social structures, the social ethos has remained highly conservative (women did not receive the vote until 1972), and what the diverse directors of the new Swiss cinema have in common is a concern to reveal the contradictions behind the outwardly calm façade of Swiss society.

It was precisely this cultural and social conservatism against which the filmmakers had to struggle to establish a film industry. In 1969, Tanner was already forty years old and had spent several years in self-imposed exile in Britain and France. Louis Marcorelles has described him as returning "in desperation" in 1960 to "a country which was for him the epitome of a slow but sure death," while Tanner himself adds that he "stayed there a while despite himself, but ended by become accommodated to it."[4] He returned to make a short film on the Swiss writer, C. F. Ramuz, and went on to make several other documentaries during the sixties. These include a triple-screen film for the Milan Triennale of 1962 on modern school architecture in Switzerland, a feature-length <u>cinéma-vérité</u> documentary in which a group of apprentices talk about their everyday lives, and a medium-length film on the city of Chandigarh in India which had been designed by the Swiss architect, Le Corbusier. These films already reveal the concern with the effect of environment on everyday life which would become a key issue in Tanner's feature films. Even more important for his later development, however, was the work that Tanner did for Swiss television during the sixties. He contributed to many programs but his most important works were four one-hour "film-portraits," including Dr. B., Country Doctor which won a Swiss television prize in 1968.

In working on his film and television documentaries, Tanner could draw on his involvement with the British Free Cinema movement (which is discussed below), but already he was dissatisfied with the possibilities of documentary. He was moving toward fiction "because of the process of selection and the impossibility of really showing the reality," and he has described his last television films as "completely fictionalised documents."[5] As we will see later, the experience of making Dr. B. provided the impetus for Charles, and the relationship of a television documentary to reality is a crucial factor in this film and in Messidor. Although he did briefly return to working for television during the hiatus between Jonah and Messidor, it is in his fiction films that Tanner has most fully explored the problems of representing reality that he first encountered in his documentary work.

Tanner was able to complete his move to fiction because of the final success of efforts to establish a Swiss film industry. The Swiss public had voted in 1956 in favor of financial support for a national cinema but it was not until 1962 that the government actually passed a subsidy law. This law had little immediate effect because of bureaucratic conservatism and inadequate funding, but it did provide a basis on which Tanner and his colleagues could build. In 1968 Tanner, Soutter, Goretta, and two other filmmakers founded the Groupe Cinq to make films in co-production with Swiss television. Charles was one of the first products of the group's efforts and, in its treatment of a man whose doubts about the social system are defined as "madness," it points to the way in which the new Swiss cinema is a response to a society in which "fear of change verges on schizophrenia."[6] This concern with the "madness" created by a constricted social and cultural environment is also found in Soutter's absurdist parables, like The Surveyors (1972) and The Escapade (1973), and Goretta's delicate character-studies, like The Madman (1970) and The Lacemaker (1977). Tanner's films seek to place this "madness" in a political context and to challenge the structures of everyday life which create it. Like the films of the other directors, his films are firmly rooted in "everyday" reality but reveal a mistrust of "normal" perspectives on that reality.

These French-speaking filmmakers do not, however, go as far in breaking with reality as some of their German-speaking compatriots, who also created a new cinema on the basis of the subsidy law. In the highly theatrical "baroque dream-world" created by Daniel Schmid in films like <u>Tonight or Never</u> (1972) and <u>La Paloma</u> (1974), for example, the "madness" takes over the whole structure of the films, as it does in German expressionist cinema and in certain areas of the new German cinema (Fassbinder, Syberberg). From the perspective of Tanner and Soutter, the two Swiss cinemas were divided not only by language but also by different "ways of seeing," the Germans being "obsessed with the problems of form" while the French-speaking filmmakers were "preoccupied with the problems of a certain immediate reality."[7] Tanner's explanation of this difference was that the roots of the German-speaking filmmakers were in painting whereas his roots and those of his colleagues were in television. Their experience in television led them to believe that the social "madness" could be countered not by the distorted forms of expressionism but by the development of a more adequate definition of reality and more critical forms of communication.

Despite improvements in the subsidy law in 1970, what unites both Swiss cinemas is the fact that they are necessarily poor. One French critic was astonished at the achievement of <u>Charles</u>, "this film made for twelve million old francs, poorer than if it had been made in an 'under-developed' country."[8] The contrast between Swiss affluence and the poverty of Swiss cinema has often frustrated the filmmakers but it also creates a productive tension in many of the films. The filmmakers were able "to refuse the industrial 'poker-game'" and thus to explore the contradiction between poverty and affluence as it manifested itself throughout Swiss society.[9] In 1970 Tanner expressed his confidence that, although "our production budgets are derisory, our distribution possibilities often blocked by the film brokers, ... little by little, the spectators will become concerned because they are the very subjects of our films."[10] The Swiss experience of living on "the frontier" also had implications which help to explain the appeal of these films to broader audiences, since it meant that Swiss cinema had to "start from zero, outside all cultural, industrial or commercial contexts and traditions, outside the overt or hidden pressures at work elsewhere."[11] Freddy Buache, a Swiss film critic, made a similar point when he argued that the requirements of a poor cinema had shown the new Swiss filmmakers "that it is by dealing with the details of our national life that it will be possible, ultimately, to arrive at the universal."[12]

The success of the Swiss cinema during the seventies fully justified such a positive outlook, but this very success has intensified rather than resolved the economic problems. Tanner's project of gradually expanding the scope of his films, for example, has been called into question by the fact that Jonah Who Will Be 25 in the Year 2000 was a French-Swiss co-production, using French as well as Swiss actors.[13] Jonah is, however, quite explicitly set in Switzerland, whereas Goretta's The Lacemaker was a French-German-Swiss co-production whose action takes place entirely in France. This problem of economic and cultural imperialism remains unresolved in Tanner's most recent work: Messidor was another French-Swiss co-production but its two major characters find themselves trapped within the Swiss borders; Light Years Away was a French-Swiss co-production made in English and filmed in the Republic of Ireland.

With the exception of Light Years Away, which represents a new departure in his work in many ways, all of Tanner's films use their Swiss settings as a basis for exploring social and political issues crucial to the whole capitalist system of which Switzerland is a very advanced part. Tanner is not afraid to mention details of Swiss history with which even the Swiss are unfamiliar or which they prefer to forget: the anarchist commune in the Jura mountains during the late-nineteenth century in Charles, for example, or the Swiss army crushing a strike in the streets of Geneva in 1932 in Jonah. These references contradict the image of Switzerland as a country exempt from the political tensions and violence that have troubled the rest of Europe during the last century; instead Switzerland is seen as a country that has been more successful than others in developing ideological strategies to conceal the contradictions on which its social structure is built. As Tanner suggested in a 1976 interview:

> My country has escaped history for a very long time. We have been hermetically sealed away, but now the walls are coming down.[14]

Or, as Charles Dé discovers in Charles, the mountains that separate Switzerland from the rest of Europe can no longer be seen as "the bearers of any truth nor any virtue."

The struggle to establish a Swiss film industry already implied a rejection of the historical and cultural amnesia encouraged by Swiss conservatism, and one of the tasks of Tanner's films is to bring to consciousness the repressed social realities. But, in so doing, they also present Switzerland as what Serge Le Peron has called the symbol or "unreal emblem" of the capitalist system.[15] What Tanner says of Messidor could be applied to any of the earlier films: "It is a film about Switzerland, not Switzerland per se, but more as a kind of symbol of what could happen to the rest of industrial civilisation."[16] The films are concerned not only to expose the details of an actual social reality but also to project a possible future based on the current workings of the system. They explore the methods by which the ideology of the consumer society has been imposed in Switzerland and look for ways to contest that ideology wherever it occurs.

Tanner has expressed his "personal disgust" at the city of Geneva which shows no signs of the industrial labor that makes its wealth possible, and John Berger (Tanner's friend and collaborator) has described this city as "a centre of paper work, of contracts, deals, plans, treaties, agreements, reports."[17] The replacement of industrial labor by "paper work" is an indication of the successful repression on which the post-industrial phase of capitalism depends (masking, for example, the heavy dependence of the Swiss economy on immigrant workers). Tanner's films depict Switzerland as the epitome of this social development, but they also reveal contradictions within the Swiss experience that help to focus the alienation which the system has generated everywhere. The stability and security which the ideology wishes to project is countered by what Tanner calls "a very Swiss preoccupation with the frontier," a concern which is especially intense for the French-speaking citizens who form a minority in their own country. Tanner describes Geneva as "a city of exiles" whose inhabitants are "condemned to being marginal."[18] The closeness of the frontier and the experience of exile and marginality have an unsettling effect in the films, an effect which undermines not only Swiss complacency but also the ideological structures that conceal the real social processes.

It is through grounding his films so firmly in their Swiss context that Tanner is able to deal with issues of social and personal life central to contemporary experience in the western world. The scope of the films, however, is clearly influenced by political and cinematic developments taking place outside Switzerland, and with which Tanner came into contact in the years before Charles. The most important of these were his involvement with Free Cinema and the New Left during his stay in England (1955-58), his presence in Paris at the time of the emergence of the French New Wave (1959-60), and his response to the "French Revolution" of May 1968. An examination of Tanner's points of contact with these movements will help to situate the political and cinematic strategies adopted in his films.

* * * *

Tanner worked in London at the British Film Institute and for BBC television from 1955 to 1958. His stay coincided with a period of cultural upheaval which affected all the arts and called into question the country's social and political institutions. The Suez debacle of 1956 was a traumatic confirmation of the decline of British power in the post-war world and of the failure of existing institutions to respond adequately to the new situation. The mood of the times was perhaps most fully expressed in John Osborne's Look Back in Anger, which (also in 1956) exploded like a bombshell in the genteel world of British theater. Jimmy Porter struck a vital nerve with his angry invective against a complacent middle-class culture in which "there aren't any good, brave causes left."[19] The play's insistently drab and vulgar realism was to have a profound effect on the development of British drama, but

other possible responses were available to theatergoers in
1956: this was also the year in which Londoners first saw
Beckett's Waiting for Godot and Brecht's Berliner Ensemble.

The developments which most immediately affected
Tanner, however, were the Free Cinema movement and the
emergence of the New Left. Tanner has described the
"capital" importance of his encounter with Lindsay Anderson and the influence on him at this time of "the Anglo-Saxon or British humanistic school of film-making."[20] Although Tanner's connection to Free Cinema is most clearly
seen in Nice Time, a 17-minute documentary on Piccadilly
Circus which he and Goretta contributed to the movement's third program in 1957, the significance for his later
work stems mainly from the debate that the movement
opened up over the social and political implications of cinematic practice. As Tanner's description suggests, the positive values of Free Cinema were essentially humanistic and
liberal, and these values were asserted against "a British
cinema still obstinately class-bound" and "still reflecting a
metropolitan Southern English culture which excludes the
rich diversity of tradition and personality which is the
whole of Britain."[21] The claim is that a new and broader
national culture will emerge once the outmoded official culture (which is imposed, not traditional) has been swept
away.

The major problem faced by the movement was that
of clearly defining the alternatives to the official culture.
Free Cinema asserted "a belief in freedom, in the importance of people and in the significance of the everyday";
but the popular culture to which it bore witness, in films
like Nice Time and Anderson's O Dreamland (1953), was
seen to be impoverished and insignificant.[22] Jimmy Porter's frustration derives from the same dilemma but, whereas he lashes out verbally against his environment, the
Free Cinema films aim at a restrained lyricism and refuse
to make dogmatic statements. The films generally do not
engage with the problem of defining their audience, given
their opposition to official culture and their disengagement
from popular culture, although the problem is raised in
one of the movement's manifestoes:

> ... is it not time that artists whose convictions
> are humanist started to consider a little more

seriously their relationship with their audience, the kind of use that can be best made of these mass media, so that their art be neither exclusive and snobbish, nor stereotyped and propagandist--but vital, illuminating, personal and refreshing?[23]

Although the films do in many ways embody the qualities advocated here, the problem of the relationship with an audience created many unresolved contradictions.

These contradictions can be illustrated from Anderson's Every Day Except Christmas (1957) (shown in the same program as Nice Time) and Karel Reisz's We Are the Lambeth Boys (1958). The former deals with the nightly work that goes into supplying and setting up Covent Garden market. It celebrates this work and creates an image of a harmonious industrial process reminiscent of such Griersonian documentaries as Drifters (1929) and Night Mail (1936), and of the sense of community projected by the wartime documentaries of Humphrey Jennings. At its first screening, however, the film produced a shock-effect which Louis Marcorelles attributes to its use of direct sound:

> The voices of porters and stallholders at Covent Garden could be heard, sometimes using crude words like 'bloody,' which until then had been banned from the polite British screens....[24]

Yet the stress in the film is on the images captured by the "candid camera" and mediated through the authoritative voice of a commentator, and Anderson has himself described his concern to limit the role of direct sound so as to create an "idealized, poetic, romanticized view of work."[25] As Elizabeth Sussex has shown, the film is completely devoid of "class-consciousness," and even its "freedom" is called into question by Anderson's willingness to introduce close-ups of the Ford insignia on the vehicles in deference to his sponsor.[26]

Similar problems arise in We Are the Lambeth Boys in which the directness of approach promised by the title is only partially realized. The film deals with the members of a youth club, but the emptiness of their lives in a world

of limited opportunities emerges virtually in spite of the
patronizing tone of the commentator. At one point, during
a communal discussion of capital punishment, he intervenes
to inform us of the need for knowledge to support opinions,
and then asks who will provide the teenagers with this
knowledge. This is a pertinent quesiton, but nowhere
does the film attempt to answer it, and the unquestioned
presence of the authoritative commentator works against
the involvement created by the use of direct sound.

The implied authors of these "personal" films are
situated outside the social contexts which they examine
and also outside, but in an uneasy relationship with, the
official culture. By refusing to acknowledge the ideological implications of their mode of address, the films develop a contradictory discourse that parallels the contradictions in the ideology that informs them. The problems
of point-of-view are more successfully negotiated in the
feature films which many of the Free Cinema filmmakers
went on to direct. Although these films do not resolve
the social dilemmas evident in the Free Cinema films, the
conventions of fictional realism--if only by doing away
with the need for an omniscient commentator--provided
a certain coherence and consistency. As in the case of
the plays and novels of the "Angry Young Man" school
on which the films were based, there is little attempt at
formal innovation but, rather, a concern to revitalize the
existing conventions by applying them to areas of reality
which had previously been ignored.

In films like Tony Richardson's adaptation of Look
Back in Anger (1958), Reisz's Saturday Night and Sunday
Morning (1960), and Anderson's This Sporting Life (1963),
the protagonists rebel against the drabness and hypocrisy
of the consumer society but, in the absence of any viable
social alternatives, can express their rebellion only in
their sexual lives. Their social frustrations, however,
poison their sexuality, and the films become studies of
ideological traps created by a society which embodies the
negation of those values promoted by the Free Cinema
manifestoes, one that fosters neither freedom nor individuality and which renders everyday life meaningless and
dispiriting. What gives the films their impact is their directness of language, challenging audiences by the use of
regional accents which contest the dominance of "metro-

politan Southern English culture." They insist on a cultural diversity suppressed by official cultural institutions and on physical realities equally suppressed by middle-class morality; although they did not develop a new political or cinematic language, they at least effectively exploited the possibilities of new accents suggested by films like Every Day Except Christmas.

The social vision of British cinema in the early sixties testifies to what Raymond Williams defines as "a continuing sense of deadlock" in contemporary British society, deriving from the conflict between "individual mobility" and "the stability of institutions and ways of thinking."[27] Williams and his colleagues in the New Left were seeking to break this deadlock by developing a new kind of socialism that could respond to the needs of modern society and close the growing gap between personal and political experience. They saw this gap as resulting from the failure of the Labour Party, which "seemed to be capitulating completely to consumer capitalism," to create "a different version of community, a pattern of new consciousness."[28] The concerns of the New Left and of Free Cinema were initially close enough for Anderson and Reisz to publish articles in Universities and Left Review and for this journal to organize screenings of Free Cinema films outside London. But the alliance collapsed, according to Alan Lovell, because of "Free Cinema's suspicion of theories and ideas"; Anderson complained that the New Left quickly degenerated into "a new generation of politicians or a new generation of academic theorists."[29]

The breakdown of the links between the New Left and Free Cinema confirmed that separation of theory and practice which was already built into British cultural life. Both groups were suspicious of dogma but, in the case of Free Cinema, this suspicion hardened into a rejection of theory that prevented any real challenge to the existing ideological structures. Although Tanner gained his first experience as a filmmaker through Free Cinema, the concerns of his later films are much closer to those of the New Left. What he may have drawn from his experience in Britain is an awareness of the need for a theoretical perspective from which to view reality and, in particular, of the need to theorize the film's relationship with its audience. The use of commentators in his films raises just those questions suppressed in the use of omniscient commentators in the Free Cinema films. Free Cinema and the New Left did agree that the site of the struggle for "a pattern of new consciousness" was everyday life, and Tanner's films are built on this conviction. In his working out of the consequent problems of realism and of relating personal to political life, Tanner's work draws very close to that of Williams, but is also very clearly affected by the writings of John Berger (whose work is closely related to the New Left), whom he met during his stay in London.

*   *   *   *

Tanner had to leave Britain in 1958 when he was unable to renew his work permit. During 1959 and 1960 he worked in various minor capacities on commercial productions in Paris, but he does not seem to have come into close contact with the New Wave directors whose films were making a powerful impact at this time. His attitude towards the New Wave is explained in a 1982 interview in which he compares his experiences in Britain and in France:

> In Paris there was the nouvelle vague, of course, but I was much more in sympathy with what was going on in London, ideologically speaking. People who were involved with the New Left Review and the Free Cinema movement were much more to my taste than those involved in the nouvelle vague who, at the time, were basically right wing anarchists.[30]

In an earlier interview, however, Tanner implies a more positive response to his period in France when he says that, after leaving Britain, he realized "what was missing in the English approach": "the English lacked the theoretical and dialectical approach to life and its problems which the French have."[31] Although Tanner clearly did not see the New Wave as the ideal outcome of the French approach, the debate that developed over the movement's challenge to French cultural values raised political and cinematic issues with which his films would be vitally concerned.

Despite the differences defined by Tanner, there were points of contact between the Free Cinema and New

Wave movements. In fact, the fifth Free Cinema program
in 1958 was entitled "French Renewal" and consisted of
François Truffaut's Les Mistons (1957) and Claude Chabrol's Le Beau Serge (1958). Both movements asserted
the need for a "personal" cinema to combat the impersonal
structures of stultified national film industries, and both
stressed the importance of the director as the source of
this cinematic personality. The attitudes that shaped
Free Cinema were initially expressed in the journals Sequence and Sight and Sound, while the New Wave directors had prepared the ground for their films by their work
as critics for Cahiers du cinéma under the influence of
André Bazin. It was Bazin's writings on film aesthetics,
with their emphasis on personal visions of reality privi-
leging deep-focus and long takes, that provided the theoretical basis missing from the British movement and allowed the French filmmakers to be more successful in
finding alternative strategies to those of the dominant
film culture.

The major difference between the British and French
approaches was immediately perceived as a question of the
relationship of form and content. The Free Cinema manifestoes tended to suggest that the problems of form would
resolve themselves once those of content had been overcome, and it was from a similar perspective that Richard
Roud, writing in Sight and Sound in 1960, took the new
French cinema to task for its "insistence on the supremacy
of form over content."[32] He contrasted Chabrol's stated
preference for "little themes" with the British belief that
a "good" subject is one that is "noble, humanistic, socially
aware, humanitarian," but he also admitted that the best
New Wave films did, apparently despite themselves, correspond to "what we in England like to think of as great
cinema: a fusion of significant form with literary or humanistic content."[33] Roud's article relates French formalism to the admiration for Hollywood films which led the
Cahiers critics to discover personal styles inflecting the
formulas of genre films and to ignore (argued Roud) the
lack of substance in these films. Although Anderson had
written a pioneer monograph on John Ford in 1955, Hollywood was firmly identified in Britain with the mass-pro-
duced popular culture that the Free Cinema films decried.

The aesthetic implications of this difference in attitude can be suggested by comparing the Free Cinema assertion that "an attitude means a style" with Luc Moullet's equally gnomic "ethics are a question of tracking shots."[34] The achievement of the New Wave can be seen as a function of the enthusiasm with which the directors explored and tested this critical principle. In describing his transition from critic to filmmaker, Jean-Luc Godard declared in 1962 that "instead of writing criticism, I make a film, but the critical dimension is subsumed."[35] A film like Breathless (1959) demonstrates that the formal strategies adopted by the filmmaker determine the ways in which a spectator can engage with the film and thus that "vision" includes both form and content. Instead of the "fusion" of "significant form" with a content, "literary or humanistic," which comes from elsewhere, the New Wave sees the initial separation of form and content as artificial and focuses attention on the ways in which reality is perceived. The implied author no longer claims to know or see more than the spectator, with the result that the narrative and visual structures of New Wave films tend to stress discontinuity and fragmentation rather than fusion.

These cinematic strategies owe much to the theoretical perspective provided by Bazin, although the New Wave vision of a fragmented world conflicts with Bazin's view of reality as a mysterious but unified totality. As Tanner's rejection of the political outlook of the New Wave suggests, however, the theoretical framework did not resolve the social and political dilemmas already encountered by the Free Cinema filmmakers. The major opposition to the political tendencies of the New Wave came from critics writing for the film journal Positif. They saw the stress on perception as an outgrowth of Bazin's essentially religious view of the world as a collection of physical appearances given meaning by underlying spiritual and eternal values. Bazin praises directors, like the Italian neorealists, who respect the mystery and ambiguity of reality so that the hidden order of things can shine through the transparency of the medium. Gérard Gozlan attacked this position in Positif in 1962, arguing that Bazin's "system can be summed up as follows: "its starting-point is the ontology of the cinema, its essence, and for convenience's sake it brushes aside such aspects as History, Economics, Politics, Technique, Society, etc."[36]

According to Gozlan, Bazin's locating of this "essence" in a cinema of deep-focus and long takes is based on the presupposition that the spectator is "virgin soil," not a being in history and society.[37] Bazin's attitude is contrasted with that of Brecht:

> The Brechtian spectacle defines the how and why of the situation it describes; it is an effort to reveal the true organisation of society and expose its contradictions. It requires a demonstration, a 'dismantling', to make the spectator grasp this.... Brecht is never ambiguous. That is why not only conservatives but 'liberals' hate him.[38]

As we will see in the next chapter, the conflict between Bazin and Brecht became a major factor in the debate over cinematic realism and in the development of Tanner's aesthetic. Gozlan does, however, underestimate the critical element in the New Wave films, which, as we have seen, develop a vision of reality as a series of fragments that need to be pieced together. Editing plays an important role in the expression of this vision, and the tensions between long takes and editing become a key element in the very different practices of all the New Wave filmmakers.

In some ways the Positif line comes very close to the argument developed by Roud, as when Robert Benayoun describes the New Wave as an "escape into formalism."[39] But what the debate most clearly reveals is a breakdown in traditional ways of defining the cinematic and its relationship to the political. As Godard put it in 1962:

> There were two kinds of values: true and false. Cahiers came along saying that the true were false and the false were true. Today there is neither true nor false, and everything has become much more difficult.[40]

In responding to this "difficult" situation, Tanner's political perspective corresponds more closely to that of the Positif critics than to that of the New Wave filmmakers. His cinema is based on a rejection of the codes of Hollywood cinema and on a radical critique of the idea of the "personal" which underlay the New Wave films. Yet his films do develop the critical element that is central to the New Wave films and are grounded in a tension between long takes and editing which builds on certain aspects of the New Wave vision.

* * * *

Before Tanner was able to make his own feature films, however, the "difficult" relationship of cinematic to political practices was given an even greater urgency by the events of May 1968. Tanner went to Paris to cover the situation for Swiss television, and the "revolution" and the issues it raised deeply affected him. When he made <u>Charles</u>, he described himself as having been "awakened" by the experiences of May.[41] The difficulties involved in keeping alive the spirit of May in a hostile environment are central to all of Tanner's films. John Berger has described the political context in which the films were made:

> In 1968, hopes, nurtured more or less underground for years, were born in several places in the world and given their names; and in the same year, these hopes were categorically defeated.... The road was cleared for what, later, would be called <u>normalization</u>.[42]

The idea of "normalization" is explicitly confronted in <u>The Middle of the World</u>, but the reality of the defeated hopes of May is explored in all the films. Tanner saw the events of May 1968 as "a great street-theatre" and argued that "what matters, much more than 'the events', is the fall-out, precisely to the extent that this theatre put hopes on stage and brought out hidden desires which have remained on the surface."[43]

Tanner's cinema tries to keep the hopes and desires of May on the surface, and a brief account of the issues at stake in the French confrontation will help to situate the politics of the films. The "events" began with a dispute between students and administration in the Paris universities and quickly escalated into mass demonstrations and a general strike that came close to toppling de Gaulle and his government. Even though the system was able to withstand the challenge, the May movement exposed and called into question the social and cultural structures of modern capitalist society. It not only attacked the establishment but also the ideological apparatus which allowed the state to define the terms and limits within which opposition was tolerated. As one participant put it, May represented "an explosion of consciousness which took place outside the current political terms of reference."[44] This was its theoretical strength and its practical weakness: the "revolution" failed partly because of the inflexibility of existing left-wing organizations, like the French Communist Party, and partly because the movement itself was "too hostile to political organisation to transform itself into an instrument for the seizure of power."[45] As a result of the experience of May, the questions of "form and content" which had remained largely on an aesthetic plane during the debate over the New Wave now took on an urgent political dimension.

One of the major problems in May was to find a satisfactory revolutionary model: the Russian revolution had been contaminated by Stalinism; the more recent revolutionary struggles (China, Cuba, Vietnam) that attracted many of the students had taken place in Third-World countries and could not be easily adapted to the French context (as Godard had shown in La Chinoise, 1967); and the parallels that were drawn with previous French revolutions (1789, 1848, 1871) were of tactical rather than ideological importance. The difficulty of creating a revolution in a society of abundance meant that the spirit of May was often seen as a kind of "madness":

> When the first workers laid down their tools at Renault, the foreman said incredulously, 'You are mad.' So they were; in turning the world topsy-turvy; in refusing to accept the ordinary and in acting out the extraordinary where the drama and the play became reality and the old reality retreated back into the shadows....[46]

But the questions posed by May were based on the assumption that the real madness was in the nature of everyday life in contemporary, technological society. They were questions that ranged from urban development to "the relationship of the subject to knowledge and truth," but, above all, they were questions that insisted that such issues cannot be separated as they were in the increasingly specialized academic and political discourses.[47]

This insistence on the relatedness of apparently separate areas of experience enabled the May movement to expose the function of ideology to create an illusory coherence which concealed the actual fragmentation and division on which the consumer society is based. The movement proposed a strategy of "contestation" to counter the ideological process of "accommodation" by which the state neutralized opposition to its values: "the accommodation of the young to the old, of socialism to capitalism and vice versa, of human relations to the inhumanity of exploitation, etc."[48] Contestation involved not only stripping away ideological masks but also the simultaneous creation of new structures:

> A truly revolutionary movement must not only challenge existing social values and structures but must in a parallel movement create the embryo of the new society to which it aspires. It must destroy and create at the same time. Otherwise the movement will run the risk of eventually conforming to the structures it is combating.[49]

To achieve this difficult task, what was needed was a new "language" that could challenge the ideological connotations that contaminated the existing languages. Thus, at the level of verbal language, the aphoristic slogans of May played with linguistic and logical codes in order to contest the fixed categories and unquestioned values of official discourses.

This contestation of "official" language was linked to an exposure of its central role in the process by which the consumer society defined reality. "Take your dreams for reality" and "Be realistic, ask for the impossible" were two of the slogans which challenged the limits of "realism" and pointed to the frustration of "desire" on which these limits depended. The liberation of desire became one of the key demands of the movement:

> A generation faced with a world based on __having__, rose to defend its right to exist in terms of __being__. What this generation has rejected is the mere satisfaction of needs which would deny them any possibility of retaining authentic and valid desire.[50]

The rejection of the passive situation of the consumer was evident throughout the events of May and it extended even to the movement's attitude to the sources on which it drew in its search for alternative structures. "Do not consume Marx" was another of the slogans.

The ideological manipulation of language to create illusion and channel desire was seen to operate at all levels of human experience. But nowhere could it be seen more clearly than in the institution of the cinema, which had developed as an industry dedicated to spectacle and illusion. The Estates General of the French Cinema was set up during May to find industrial and aesthetic strategies to counter those of the dominant cinema. Hollywood, and those national cinemas that could afford to compete, spent vast sums of money to create an illusion of reality and had developed a set of techniques and conventions that ensured that this illusion would not be broken. The spectator was encouraged to identify with well-known stars and to see what was on the screen as a projection of his/her own fantasies. Since this process was presented as "natural" or neutral, the film could deny that it carried any ideological implications and the spectator could be constituted as an untroubled voyeur. In other words, the "Hollywood system" was designed to create films that were easy to consume. Thus the projects developed by the Estates General stressed the need for an approach that would "make possible a more active role for the spectator: the role of challenging, analysing and criticising the spectacle, not simply consuming it."[51]

With cinema, as with so many aspects of the May movement, the goal was clear but there was widespread debate over how to achieve it. The effect of May on Cahiers du cinéma, for example, was to provoke a radical shift from auteur-based analyses to a critical engagement with the workings of ideology. Whereas the auteurists had sought for the signs of an authorial presence beneath the codes and conventions imposed by the system, their successors rejected what they now saw as a romantic cult of the author in favor of a concern with the ideological strategies of the text. The stress on "language" within the May movement made it possible to unmask these strategies. Cahiers insisted that "every film is political, inasmuch as it is determined by the ideology which produces it," and that "only action on both fronts, 'signified' and 'signifier,' has any hope of operating against the prevailing ideology."[52] The implications of this coupling of linguistic terminology with ideological analysis are discussed in the next chapter, but the argument is in fact a radical version of the basic argument of the politique des auteurs: that meaning is conveyed by "form" as well as by "content." To the Cahiers critics of 1968 this meant that a radical filmmaker could not make a radical film without completely abandoning the ideologically contaminated language of the dominant cinema.

Other ("reformist"?) elements within the May movement did argue for the modification of "popular" forms to make the political issues easily accessible to large audiences, but there was a strong feeling that effective contestation required avant-garde works that could not be comfortably consumed. The effect of this position can be seen in the career of Godard, whose pre-May films--La Chinoise, Weekend (1967), Le Gai Savoir (1968)--had shown themselves increasingly hostile to bourgeois society and to the codes of its cinema. After May, Godard submerged his personal identity in the Dziga Vertov collective which produced extremely challenging films that tried to develop a new cinematic language appropriate to new political values. Despite their didactic intentions, the Dziga Vertov films often adopt an intensely questioning and self-critical stance with regard to both cinematic and political discourse, and Godard's later works bear witness to the unresolved problems involved in the spectator's relationship to the film.

In Tout va bien (1972), for example, Godard and Jean-Pierre Gorin tried to create a film that would be more accessible than the Dziga Vertov films but that would still articulate the political issues raised by May. The film acknowledges its uneasy relationship to the commercial cinema in its opening sequence in which checks to cover its cost are signed. It has two stars (Yves Montand, Jane Fonda) and a narrative built around a "love story." However, many more distancing devices follow the check-signing and prevent the spectator from passively consuming the film. A revival of the spirit of May in the occupation of a factory by its workers provides the catalyst for the characters' reassessment of their lives after May and their accommodation into the system through their jobs, he as a filmmaker who has chosen to make advertising films because he feels this

is more honest than trying to adapt the lessons of May to
the demands of the film industry, she as a radio journalist
who finds that her reports are censored.

The impasse reached by his characters and the controversy surrounding Godard's continuing attempts to evolve new cinematic (and televisual) forms suggest that the question of "form and content" is still very much an open one. Whereas Godard said in 1962 that "everything has become much more difficult," the effect of May was to place this difficulty in a political context by demonstrating that "the road to socialism is not clear."[53] In 1969 Godard (from within the Dziga Vertov group) sought to respond to these difficulties in British Sounds, which begins with a fist punching through a paper Union Jack and a voice declaring, "The bourgeoisie created a world in its image. Comrades, let us destroy that image." In attempting to break down ideological structures, the filmmakers constantly subvert the conventional relationship of sound and image, as in the first sequence which consists of a tracking shot along an assembly line in a car factory while a voice (often inaudible) recites passages from the Communist Manifesto.

The opposite extreme to this deconstructive strategy can be represented by Costa-Gavra's Z (also 1969), which uses the generic "form" of the thriller in an attempt to expose popular audiences to the political methods of the Greek military dictatorship. Tanner's response to the cinematic and political difficulties foregrounded by the failure of the May revolution was neither to break completely with existing cinematic models nor to adapt the "popular" genres to new political ends. Instead, from Charles (in 1969) onwards, he attempts to build on the example of the New Wave, questioning rather than celebrating the autonomy of the individual personality and placing his formal strategies within a context of ideological analysis. His concern is to create films that are neither so difficult that their audience must be severely limited, nor so easy that they can be comfortably consumed. In fact, he aims to build on the tensions between these two poles to develop a cinema that can both challenge and create pleasure and that can question existing "languages" without losing touch with potential audiences. The films do not assume an audience that is ready-made (whether by political conviction or familiarity with conventions); rather, they seek to create and to build their own audiences through a process of critical interaction between spectator and film.

Developing the concern with social reality of the Free Cinema, the critical focus of the New Wave, and the ideological awareness of May 1968, Tanner's cinema explores the cinematic and political dilemmas of his culture in order to encourage critical awareness in audiences. In doing so, it also takes a critical stance towards the conventions of realism as well as towards the structuralist theories that were undermining the foundations of realist art. The implications of these issues for Tanner's films are taken up in the next chapter.

NOTES

1. For a brief account of the history and development of the Swiss film industry see James Monaco, "Swiss Cinema," in Richard Roud, ed., Cinema: A Critical Dictionary (London: Secker and Warburg, 1980), vol. II, pp. 996-1000; for Tanner's account of the development of the new Swiss cinema see "Alain Tanner: Charles mort ou vif," Cahiers du cinéma, 213, June 1969, pp. 26-30.

2. Graham Greene and Carol Reed, The Third Man (New York: Simon and Schuster, 1968), p. 114n.

3. "Conversation avec Michel Soutter et Alain Tanner," in André Pâquet, ed., Jeune cinéma suisse (Montreal: La Bibliothèque nationale du Québec, 1970), p. 34.

4. Louis Marcorelles, "Situation I," in Pâquet, p. 3; Alain Tanner, "Biofilmographie," in L'Avant-scène du cinéma, 108, p. 37.

5. Michael Tarantino, "Alain Tanner: After Jonah," Sight and Sound, Winter 1978/9, p. 43.

6. Tanner, "Situation 2," in Pâquet, p. 5.

7. Soutter and Tanner, in Pâquet, p. 35.

8. Philippe Haudiquet, "Un Enfant du mois de mai," in *L'Avant-scène du cinéma*, 108, p. 9.

9. Marcorelles, p. 4.

10. Tanner, in Pâquet, p. 6.

11. "Entretien avec Alain Tanner," *Cahiers du cinéma*, 273, January-February 1977, p. 38.

12. Freddy Buache, "Situation 3," in Pâquet, p. 8.

13. This issue is addressed in the film *Cinema Dead or Alive*, made by the Filmcollectif Zurich during the shooting of *Jonah*.

14. Renee Epstein, "Conversation with Alain Tanner," *Soho Weekly News*, 4 November 1976, quoted in Andrew Horton, "*Jonah*...: Echoes of Renoir's *M. Lange*," *Film Criticism*, vol. IV, no. 3, p. 25.

15. Serge Le Peron, "Ici ou ailleurs," *Cahiers du cinéma*, 273, January-February 1977, p. 45.

16. Tarantino, p. 40.

17. Tanner, *Cahiers*, 213, p. 30; John Berger, *A Seventh Man* (New York: Viking Press, 1975), p. 153.

18. Jill Forbes, "Interview with Alain Tanner," *Films and Filming*, February 1982, p. 22.

19. John Osborne, *Look Back in Anger* (London: Faber and Faber, 1957), p. 84; the first production of the play was directed by Tony Richardson, who was also a leading figure in the Free Cinema movement and the director of the film based on the play.

20. Tanner, "Biofilmographie," p. 37; and "Alain Tanner: Isolation and Ennui," *Film*, July 1975, p. 18.

21. Introduction to the third Free Cinema program (which included *Nice Time*), quoted in Elizabeth Sussex, *Lindsay Anderson* (London: Studio Vista, 1969), p. 32.

22. Free Cinema manifesto, quoted in Sussex, p. 31.

23. Sussex, p. 32.

24. Louis Marcorelles, Living Cinema, trans. Isabel Quigly (New York: Praeger Publishers, 1973), p. 42; the relationship of Free Cinema to earlier documentary movements is discussed in Gavin Lambert, "Free Cinema," Sight and Sound, Spring 1956, p. 177.

25. Anderson, quoted in Marcorelles, p. 44; and Joseph Gelmis, ed., The Film Director as Superstar (New York: Doubleday, 1970), p. 97.

26. Sussex, p. 35.

27. Raymond Williams, The Long Revolution (London: Chatto and Windus, 1961), p. 244.

28. Raymond Williams, Politics and Letters (London: New Left Books, 1979), p. 364; and The Long Revolution, p. 333.

29. Alan Lovell, "Free Cinema," in Alan Lovell and Jim Hillier, Studies in Documentary (London: Secker and Warburg, 1972), p. 155; and Anderson, quoted in Lovell, p. 156.

30. Forbes, p. 21.

31. Tanner, "Isolation and Ennui," p. 18.

32. Richard Roud, "The French Line," Sight and Sound, Autumn 1960, p. 167.

33. Claude Chabrol, "Little Themes," in Peter Graham, ed., The New Wave (London: Secker and Warburg, 1968), pp. 73-7; Roud, pp. 167, 170.

34. Luc Moullet, quoted by Robert Benayoun, "The King Is Naked," in Graham, p. 169.

35. "Interview with Jean-Luc Godard," Cahiers du cinéma, 138, December 1962, in Tom Milne, ed., Godard on Godard (London: Secker and Warburg, 1972), p. 171.

36. Gérard Gozlan, "In Praise of André Bazin," in Graham, p. 132.
37. Gozlan, p. 58.
38. Gozlan, p. 126.
39. Benayoun, p. 172.
40. Godard, p. 195.
41. Tanner, quoted by Haudiquet, p. 8.
42. John Berger, About Looking (New York: Pantheon Books, 1980), p. 127.
43. Tanner, Cahiers, 273, p. 42.
44. Quoted in Y.L., "The May Movement at the Lycée Pasteur, Neuilly," in Charles Posner, ed., Reflections on the Revolution in France: 1968 (Harmondsworth: Penguin Books, 1970), p. 136.
45. Alain Touraine, quoted in Sylvia Harvey, May '68 and Film Culture (London: British Film Institute, 1978), p. 10.
46. Posner, p. 50.
47. Maud Mannoni, "Psychoanalysis and the May Revolution," in Posner, p. 224.
48. André Glucksmann, "Action," in Posner, p. 188.
49. Jean-Pierre Vigier, "The Action Committees," in Posner, p. 205.
50. Mannoni, pp. 219-20.
51. Harvey, p. 24; for the projects emerging from the Estates General, see "The Estates General of the French Cinema, May 1968," Screen, Winter 1972/73, pp. 58-88.
52. Jean-Luc Comolli and Jean Narboni, "Cinema/Ideology/Criticism," in Bill Nicholls, ed., Movies and Methods

(Berkeley: University of California Press, 1976), pp. 24, 26.

53. Daniel Singer, Prelude to Revolution: France in May 1968 (New York: Hill and Wang, 1970), p. 366.

2: CIRCLE AND MARGIN: TANNER IN THEORY

> Under the cover of the congenital realism of the cinematographic image, a complete system of abstraction has been fraudulently introduced. One believes limits have been set by breaking up the events according to a sort of anatomy natural to the action: in fact one has subordinated the wholeness of reality to the 'sense' of the action. One has transformed nature into a series of 'signs.'
> --André Bazin[1]

> The association of signs, whether it be strong or weak, is what distinguishes us humans from the other animals. Rather, it is what makes us complex, problematical, and unpredictable beings.
> --Octavio Paz[2]

The situation in which Tanner found himself after May 1968 was an extremely complex one. If the New Wave had exposed the limitations of the direct relationship of film to reality assumed by Free Cinema, the upheavals of May had confirmed the remoteness of the New Wave from the most urgent political and social issues of the day. The "invisible," psychological editing of the classical realist cinema that had been the object of Bazin's attack continued to dominate popular cinema and television. Yet Bazin's own version of realism, with its respect for the "ambiguity" and "mystery" that constituted the "wholeness of reality," itself came under attack (along the lines suggested in <u>Positif</u>) for ignoring the ideological pressures that shape our responses to reality. In fact, both kinds of realism were seen to depend on a denial that what we are seeing has been constructed: classical realism by creating the illusion of continuity, Bazinian realism by creating a density of texture that can be experienced as "nature." Given the problems involved in the representation of reality, it is hardly surprising that many filmmakers, like Godard, felt that a complete break with any notion of realism was necessary if film was to find adequate ways of dealing with the "difficulties" which May had so painfully brought to light.

One of the key elements in this break with realism was the creation of a detached perspective for the spectator by the acknowledgment of the processes of the film's making and of its viewing. The spectator is not asked to respond to an illusion whose origin is unquestioned (classical realism) or to a re-creation of a mysterious reality filtered through an artist's personality (Bazin), but rather to interpret a series of signs that originate in a specified social and political context. In this way, the experience of watching the film encourages the spectator to view reality itself as a collection of signs arranged to serve certain specific purposes and subject to change if these do not satisfy human needs. Precedents for such an anti-realist stance could be found in the various "modernist" movements of the early twentieth century and, especially, in the "montage" theories of Brecht in the theater and of Eisenstein in cinema. But the dominant influence on radical film theory and practice after May 1968 came from structuralism (and the related discipline of semiotics), which analyzes the codes and signs by which what we know as reality is organized.

The contribution of the structuralist outlook to Tanner's films is evident from the beginning and has led (as in the case of many other structuralist-influenced works) to charges of coolness or schematization. The films constantly call attention to themselves as artifacts and to the sign-making process in all human activity, and they clearly subscribe to Paz's placing of this process at the core of what it means to be human. Yet Tanner is also closely related to a movement that is increasingly critical of those elements within structuralism which regard human activity as being determined by fixed and unchanging structures, often working at deeply unconscious levels. Critics of structuralism include the defenders of traditional humanist values (coupled, usually, with traditional realism) as well as various groups on the left, including the British New Left, who value some of its insights but resist its tendency to downplay the role of history and of actual experience. Tanner's films clearly contribute to this latter position.

Much of the controversy over structuralism centers on the work of Louis Althusser, the French philosopher who has attempted to re-read Marx in structuralist terms. Althusser argues that traditional humanism has been used as a screen to conceal social practices which are, in fact, inhuman and alienating, and that the central humanist concept of the "human subject" is simply an illusion created by a "structure of misrecognition" developed by bourgeois ideology.[3] The effect of Althusser's structuralism, his critics argue, is to reinforce those tendencies in modern, corporate society which the May revolution was directed against, and which treat people as ciphers and statistics within a monolithic system. Thus Henri Lefebvre, the Marxist sociologist quoted by Tanner at the end of Charles, has repeatedly attacked structuralism for placing "the accent on stability and permanence," contrary to the Marxist stress on historical change and dialectical analysis; while Yves Velan has related structuralism to "technocratic ideology" because it "presupposes that meaning is no longer to be sought, that society is given, and that the only problem is to manipulate it as it is."[4]

Tanner's cinema is firmly opposed to this "technocratic ideology," but this does not lead to a complete rejection of structuralism. The implicit problem addressed by all the films is that of how to re-think the "human" without losing sight of the structuralist perspective on the functioning of social and cultural codes. Tanner's response is to explore the human capacity for making signs, developing Paz's definition of human nature. His films show people making their own structures, as well as being prevented from doing so by existing social structures. These structures are both social (modern business methods in Charles, provincial politics in The Middle of the World) and perceptual, the ingrained "ways of seeing" that our culture makes seem "natural." Tanner feels that both kinds of structure must be attacked at the same time: thus the male writers in The Salamander search for, and fail to find, an adequate structure that would allow them to articulate the problems of a female worker confronted with the oppressive social structures of the workplace; similarly, the couple in Return from Africa gain a new perspective on their social environment as a result of their imaginary journey to Africa.

This concern with structural process and perceptual

structures takes Tanner away from the mainstream of structuralism. Edward L. Said has objected that what structuralism cannot do is "to show us why structure structures; structure is always revealed in the condition of having structures, but never ... structuring, or in the condition of being structured, or failing to structure."[5] The effect of Tanner's films is to demystify the notion of structure by showing that all structures are temporary and subject to change, becoming permanent only when their origins have been forgotten or suppressed. While their structuralist perspective allows the films to challenge certain habitual ways of seeing and thinking, they resist the tendency of structural thought itself to become habitual through their focus on contradictions between and within structures. In so doing, they re-define structuralism in terms suggested by E. P. Thompson, the New Left historian, in his long and detailed attack on Althusser. Although Thompson feels that Althusser's preference for "a structured whole, within which process is encapsulated" taints the whole structuralist endeavor, he does suggest an alternative approach which is close to Tanner's and which would work in terms of "a structured process, which, while subject to determinate pressures, remains open-ended and only partially determined."[6]

Whereas Althusser's structuralism tends towards a position that sees "cultural struggle within capitalism as theoretically inconceivable," Tanner's cinema assumes the possibility of change from within the cinematic and social structures that it contests.[7] "My position," he said just before he began shooting Messidor, "is not to be as radical as Godard, but to try to force the commercial world to open their doors to outside experiences."[8] This position is a difficult one, requiring as it does a constant awareness of and resistance to strong forces pulling in different directions, and Tanner admitted (even after having made five feature films) that he was not sure if the strategy would work. It involves a calculated risk of the kind suggested by Brecht's argument that, since cultural forms must change along with social structures, "there is not only such a thing as being popular, there is also the process of becoming popular."[9] For Godard, as for Althusser, this means that cultural forms must lead the way (that is, function as an avant-garde), but for Tanner the relationship between cultural forms and social structures is a complex and dialectical one in which each must respond to the other.

The tensions inherent in this position are basically those described by Tanner in defining the situation of the characters in Jonah:

> They are marginals 'on the inside.' If one draws a circle which would contain the social body, they are certainly situated on the margin, but this margin is inside the circle. The wind which blows the fall-out from 68 always blows towards the exterior, towards the outside. We wanted to reverse this movement so that the seeds it carries would fall inside.[10]

To be completely marginal, outside the circle, is to be powerless, like Paul and Adeline in Charles, who have deprived themselves of all possibility of "a true political engagement or of finding other forms of contestation."[11] To be in the center of the circle is to lack the detachment necessary to identify the sources of oppression, as Charles himself discovers in running his watch factory.

The struggle of the characters to remain inside the circle while resisting the pull to the center is paralleled in the style and structure of Tanner's films. Unlike Godard, Tanner has been concerned "to avoid discourses that were too marked in order not to go outside the circle."[12] This strategy has frequently been condemned as insufficiently radical. As early as 1969, Tanner noted that some young critics and filmmakers in Switzerland felt that the new Swiss cinema had already been "assimilated by the system" and were taking up what Tanner considered a "very marginal" position by making 8mm. "underground" films.[13] In the United States, the editors of Jump Cut attacked Jonah for concealing behind its "charm" a reactionary attitude to women, foreign workers, and the Swiss working class, and concluded that Tanner was adopting a "position within mainstream bourgeois filmmaking."[14] Tanner has responded to such charges by insisting that he is not interested in holding up "a mirror" in which groups on "the extreme left" can "admire themselves," and by attributing their attitude to their refusal "to look at the images."[15] The films refuse to resolve the problems of the relationship of cinematic to political practice but, through their strategy of resisting both centrifugal and centripetal pressures, they seek to create a field of tensions which must be related to the spectator's own situation.

* * * *

Tanner's concern to stay inside the circle involves a confrontation with the codes and conventions of realism. In this respect, his work is closely related to that of Raymond Williams, the critic and novelist who has been a leading figure in the New Left movement. Williams' position on structuralism is very close to that implied by Tanner's films; he feels that "the hypothesis of a <u>structure</u> ... can encourage clarification of fundamental relationships, often of a kind screened by assumption or habit," but warns against the tendency to see "not human beings living in and through <u>structures</u>, but <u>structures</u> living in and through human beings."[16] He finds structuralism's stress on "relations" too abstract and too static to cope with the complex and dynamic "relationships" which realism at its best can discover:

> The truly creative effort of our time is the struggle for relationships, of a whole kind, and it is possible to see this as both personal and social: the practical learning of <u>extending</u> relationships.... In the highest realism, society is seen in fundamentally personal terms, and persons, through relationships, in fundamentally social terms.[17]

Williams defends this kind of realism against the modernist "rejection of realism" based on the discovery "that man lives through his perceptual world, which is a human interpretation of the world outside him." Without denying the significance of this discovery, Williams insists that "art is more than perception; it is a particular kind of active response, and a part of all human communication."[18]

But Williams' account of realism is not only defensive: it is also directed towards the extension and renewal of the possibilities of realism. Referring to some examples from Brecht, he develops the idea of a "subjunctive mode" of realism that could present the possible as well as the actual outcomes of a situation. Traditional ("indicative") realism is limited to showing "what reality is like," and this may involve presenting "a social situation in which at one level or another all roads have been blocked; or even if certain limits are being pushed back, they will still by definition subsist so long as this class society remains"; "subjunctive" realism can go beyond this experience of "deadlock" by suggesting possibilities suppressed by the actual situation.[19] This extension of realism to include the possible or desirable is also found in the co-existence in Tanner's films of bleak social situations, in which limits can be pushed back only marginally, with elements that have been described as "utopian" (a term which Williams rejects as less suitable to his purposes than "subjunctive"). The most obvious example is the use of black-and-white inserts in Jonah to represent the desires of the characters, desires which achieve momentary reality in the "utopian" harmony of the commune only to be blocked by the actual social pressures.

The references forward to the year 2000 in Jonah also serve to relate subjunctive realism to the concern of co-screenwriter John Berger that art should address an "alternative future," a position which requires that art should "attempt to define and make unnatural" the distinction between "the actual and the desirable."[20] This distinction is basic to the critical deployment of the codes of realism and the concerns of structuralism in Tanner's films. As Todd Gitlin puts it, "the films move dialectically: as we watch, the possible is always threatening to slip out from under the actual"; and, as Robert Stam argues in his discussion of Jonah, the effect is "a redefinition of the desirable.... Jonah tries to think through the social logic of our desires even while it demystifies the political and ideological structures that channel our desires in oppressive directions."[21]

It is precisely this sense of the possible within the actual that Lefebvre finds missing in Althusser's structuralism. According to Lefebvre, there are always "in the heart of the structures, active forces which dissolve them or break them, which produce destructuration." He stresses that "the possible is not exterior to the real nor the future to the present." Tanner's concern that the "seeds" from May 1968 (when the possible briefly became the actual) should fall inside the circle can be related to Lefebvre's argument that "in society as in nature, there are germs which bear the future and virtualities which emerge according to circumstances." This view of structure requires an awareness of such "germs and virtualities in the real and in the present" and a conviction that their existence "has nothing mysterious about it."[22] The extension of the idea of the real and the demystification of the structuring process, suggested from somewhat different perspectives by Williams and

34 / A Possible Cinema

Lefebvre, become key elements in the attempt of Tanner's cinema to unbalance and call into question existing social and perceptual structures.

The tensions set up in the films between the indicative and the subjunctive, the actual and the desirable, have been effectively summarized in Serge Le Peron's suggestion that the conjunction "or" is basic to Tanner's vision. Thus we are confronted with the alternatives of "the poetry of Pierre OR the rationality of Paul in The Salamander," of Charles Dead OR Alive, of Switzerland OR Africa in Return from Africa, of "the here OR elsewhere that is required by the expression Middle of the World," and of "the today OR tomorrow of Jonah." Le Peron comments that this structure allows the use of established codes which are, however, presented as "provisional," and that it creates a relationship between utopia and reality in which "the one breaks down the other and vice versa."[23] The real and the present, life at the center of the circle, impose burdens which it is tempting to reject outright but (as many of Tanner's characters find) this leads to isolation and impotence. Contact with the social and perceptual structures that emanate from the center is necessary to provide a context within which desire can be defined and have an effect.

One earlier movement which sought to inject desire into the real was surrealism, and Tanner's debt to the surrealist perspective has often been noted. The aim of surrealism, according to Max Ernst, was to revolutionize "the relationship between 'realities'" in order to "accelerate the general crisis of conscience and consciousness in our time."[24] A surrealist work of art makes its impact through the tensions set up between the inflexibility of established ways of seeing and the scandalous freedom of its appeal to the structures of dream and desire. Theodor Adorno suggests that "the dialectical pictures of Surrealism emerge from a dialectic of subjective freedom circumscribed by a state of objective non-freedom"; and Berger adopts a similar position in an essay on Magritte in which he argues that art is a mediation between "what is given and what is desired," that unity was possible in the past because "the contradiction between what was and what could be thought was not yet insurmountable," but that this unity becomes impossible as "our idea of freedom extends" and "our experience of it diminishes."[25] Not surprisingly, the spirit of surrealism was very much in evidence during the events of May, and its influence on Tanner's films can be seen in their concern to challenge "objective non-freedom" by activating the conflict with subjective freedom at all levels of the cinematic experience.

Despite Tanner's commitment to the surrealist goal of "the strengthening of consciousness by unsettling it," however, his films are too firmly rooted in the codes of realism to look like surrealist works.[26] They perhaps come closest to the paintings of Magritte with their subtle challenge to familiar structures of perception. But Tanner's concern with social structures leads him to anchor the desirable and the possible in the structures of everyday life. If surrealism tends to resolve the tension between the actual and the desirable in favor of the latter, and realism and structuralism have tended (in different but ultimately complementary ways) to resolve it in favor of the former, Tanner works to maintain the tension and to bring it to consciousness. The actual dominates the visual dimension of the films since it provides the material context for the action, and thus the codes of realism can be apparently respected. But the arrangement of the images constantly calls attention to their function as signs and to their place within structures, forcing us to re-evaluate the perceptual structures on which realism relies as well as the social codes which influence perception.

* * * *

Many of the strategies which Tanner adopts in his attempt to relate perception to ideology and to activate the possible within the actual clearly owe much to his collaboration with John Berger. The biographical details of their relationship are of little relevance to this study, despite the suggestion that the collaboration of Pierre and Paul in The Salamander mirrors the collaboration of Berger and Tanner on that film. But Berger's contribution to Tanner's cinema is important and closely related to its critical stance towards realism and structuralism. They first met when Tanner was working in London, and their working relationship dates back to the television documentary, A City at Chandigarh (1966), for which Berger wrote the commentary. As described by Berger, the relationship of word and image in this documentary film anticipates the strategies of the later fiction films:

> Instead of writing a descriptive commentary about the architecture, what I used were quotations from poets and political theorists which were placed in juxtaposition--sometimes ironic, sometimes confirmative--of what was seen on the screen.[27]

The use of quotations, the unpredictable interventions of a commentator, and the interplay of different levels of verbal and visual discourse, all would become central to Tanner's cinematic language, even in those films on which Berger did not formally collaborate.

Berger received credit as co-scenarist on The Salamander, The Middle of the World, and Jonah, but he also contributed to Charles and to Return from Africa. Berger says that Tanner discussed Charles with him "quite a lot," and the film has its origins in issues raised in the television documentary, Dr. B., Country Doctor (1967), which was closely related to Berger's study of an English country doctor in A Fortunate Man (published in 1967).[28] In the case of Return from Africa, Berger says that he told Tanner "the story upon which it is based" and describes the film as "a kind of unrecognized or unformulated collaboration."[29] Moreover, Berger was the English translator (with Anna Bostock) of Aimé Cesaire's long poem, Return to My Native Land, a text which figures prominently in the film. Berger has not worked with Tanner since Jonah, explaining that Tanner "was more interested in making films of a looser structure" while his own development was towards "tighter and more traditional" narrative structures.[30]

Tanner praises Berger for his "incredible ability to place things immediately, to see exactly how things fit together," and Berger agrees that his major contribution to their partnership is his "strong sense of form, of how all the parts must fit together and add up to a totality."[31] In an interview given in 1982, Tanner attributes this quality to Berger's Marxist training, since "the basic principle of dialectics is the ability to analyse the relations between things," but raises doubts as to whether he considers himself a Marxist when he seems to accept the suggestion that "Jonah isn't a Marxist film."[32] Yet he had earlier described himself as "an undogmatic Marxist," and Berger insists that, although it is for the spectator to decide if the films are Marxist, "both Alain's and my own attitude to the world and to contemporary reality are enormously influenced by Marxism."[33] Whatever the precise nature of this influence, it is clear that Tanner's contact with Berger can only have inflected his vision towards a more precise analysis of the interaction of social and perceptual structures.

Berger's sense of how things fit together has been employed in his novels mainly to delineate the experience of characters who cannot fit themselves into their social environments. The feeling of being an exile cut off from a sustaining social and cultural context is as important in Berger's work as it is in Tanner's. (Berger has lived in France since the early sixties but the figure of the exile appears in the novels written before he left England.) When the state of exile is actual, as it is for the Hungarian painter in London in Berger's A Painter of Our Time (1958), for Emilio the Spaniard who is deported from Switzerland in Return from Africa, and for the thousands of "guest workers" in Europe whose plight Berger documents in A Seventh Man (1975), at least the fact of alienation and its causes are apparent. In many cases, however, "exile" is a metaphor for an unconscious dissatisfaction caused by the gulf between people's desires and aspirations and their social and cultural institutions, and it becomes a function of the art of contestation to provoke awareness of this situation. The danger in this is that, unless the institutions change, the breakthrough to consciousness may be experienced as "madness," which the prevailing ideology sees as a failure of adaptation but which Berger defines as "revolutionary freedom confined to the self."[34]

Both Berger and Tanner are concerned to explore this kind of madness but also to find ways to go beyond it. George Szanto suggests that Berger's aim is "to tilt the commonsensical perception of the external world," and madness provides a perspective from which this can occur.[35] The difficulty involved in transforming the perspective of (personal) madness into (social) revolution becomes an issue both at the level of the narrative and at the level of the form of the work and the relationship it establishes with the reader/spectator. For Berger this difficulty is paralleled by the problem of the artist's relationship to reality: "Experience is indivisible and continuous ... the act of approaching a given moment of experience involves both scrutiny (closeness) and the capacity to connect (distance)."[36]

Berger describes the effect of continuity created by "the viewing-point of Renaissance perspective, fixed and outside the picture, but to which everything within the picture was drawn," and he stresses the importance of cubism, which replaced this perspective with "a field of vision which is the picture itself." Cubism, he argues, did not destroy Renaissance perspective but rather "broke its continuity," and his novels and Tanner's films adopt a similar strategy towards everyday perceptions of reality.[37]

The breaking of continuity is largely a matter of accepting that art transforms nature into signs, and it is here that Berger finds the historical significance of cubism. He describes the evolution of what he calls "the metaphorical model for the function of painting": in the early Renaissance the model was the mirror; from Michelangelo to the French Revolution it was the theater stage; after Rousseau, Kant and the French Revolution it was the personal account; and with cubism it became the diagram:

> ... the diagram being a visible symbolic representation of invisible processes, forces, structures. A diagram need not eschew certain aspects of appearances: but these too will be treated symbolically as signs, not as imitations or re-creations.[38]

The effect of this model is to allow the cubist artist to reveal "visually the interlocking of phenomena," and the movement thus "created the possibility in art of revealing processes instead of static states of being." Cubism is seen as "an art entirely concerned with interaction," including "the interaction between structure and movement," and its achievement as the "dynamic liberation from all static categories."[39]

Using Berger's terminology, Tanner's films can be said to incorporate elements of the models of mirror, stage, and personal account, but they are basically diagrams making visible the hidden structures that govern our lives. The model of the diagram also suggests a link with structuralism (the use of diagrams being a favorite device in structuralist analyses), which Roland Barthes has defined in similar terms:

> The goal of all structuralist activity ... is to re-

construct an 'object' in such a way as to manifest thereby the rules of functioning ... of this object. Structure is therefore actually a <u>simulacrum</u> of the object, but a directed, <u>interested</u> simulacrum, since the imitated object makes something appear which remained invisible or, if one prefers, unintelligible in the natural object. Structural man takes the real, decomposes it, then recomposes it...: the simulacrum is intellect added to object.[40]

Barthes' simulacrum functions much like Berger's diagram, and the idea of "intellect added to object" could also be applied to the critical realism of Tanner's films.

Yet, as we have seen, structuralism has rarely provided the "dynamic" sense of interaction celebrated in Berger's account of cubism and implied in the active process described by Barthes. Szanto has suggested that structuralism does contribute to Berger's work by challenging the static categories of "common-sense." Berger regards common sense as static because it belongs to the ideology of "those who are socially passive, never understanding what or who has made their situation as it is," and because it is "based on the acceptance of an outdated view of the possible."[41] According to Szanto, Berger adopts a structuralist perspective to create an awareness of ideological processes but goes beyond the limits set by "ahistorical structuralism." By using the methods of "dialectical and historical materialism," Berger presents systems as "processes of changes (perhaps even of contradiction, creation or dismantling)" and signs as "part of simultaneous and often conflicting cultures at a given moment in history (and that moment itself, like every other moment including the moment of the writing, being in a state of flux)."[42]

Such a perspective allows for an engagement with the complex relationship of structures to historical processes and for the development of critical strategies of intervention. Szanto describes Berger's work as "the exploration of some oppositional social structures and their possible daily patterns."[43] Tanner's films also try to reveal the possible within the everyday by contesting the static perspectives of both common sense and structuralism. As Michael Tarantino shows, Berger and Tanner are also necessarily involved in a contestation of the formal and narrative structures which have become part of literary or cinematic "common sense," questioning "the elements of 'domination' that are taken for granted in a text/reader relationship." Tarantino demonstrates that such devices in the films as "the use of off-screen commentary" and "the multitude of voices" relate to similar devices in Berger's novels, and that their function is to restore "the active, dialectical process to replace a consumptive one."[44]

A much fuller study could be made of the parallels and differences between the Berger and Tanner texts. But it is enough for the present purpose to suggest that both rest on the creation of a "subjunctive mode" which can open up social and artistic processes. As Szanto puts it with regard to Berger's "oppositional perspectives":

> ... he takes it as a duty of his work to show not only how oppositional social circumstances can come about, but also how a contemporary simplified understanding of a social situation has come about, and how such a situation can be unravelled so that its several parts, when no longer existing in some mysterious combination, can be understood in terms of the ideological roles they have been, and are, called upon to play.[45]

This clearly involves a structuralist separation of a system into its component parts, but also an exploration of what holds the parts together, of how and why structures structure. At a formal level, it requires that the structuring process be acknowledged along with the spectator's role in the creation of meaning. Thus, according to Tarantino, both Berger and Tanner expose "the deep structure of their works in order to open up the relationship with an audience" and foreground the paradigmatic dimension of the semiotic process so that "each choice of signifier is also a reminder that the opposing method has been rejected."[46] The reader or spectator is thus reminded of the existence of other possibilities and encouraged to intervene in the work of the narrative structures.

* * * *

The critical engagement that Tanner's films demand of the spectator also points to the influence of the Brechtian "estrangement effect." We have already seen that Williams' notion of the subjunctive mode derives from Brecht, and Tanner has admitted that "Brecht has greatly influenced me, perhaps more than I imagine."[47] What Brecht stresses in his theater of "montage" is that the events of the play should be removed from "the realm of the ordinary, natural, or expected, and function as scenes complete in themselves."[48] By "estranging" the events from their familiar contexts, the effect is to encourage the spectator to work out the possible relationships between them. As Tanner argues with regard to what he calls "the epic (in the Brechtian sense) structure" of <u>Jonah</u>, the segmentation of the narrative into "a succession of scenes closed in on themselves" not only serves to unfasten "the links of the chain" but also creates the possibility of perceiving new relationships between the different elements.[49]

The Brechtian elements in Tanner's films place his work firmly within the context of the "<u>art of conjugation</u>" envisaged by Octavio Paz (whose writings figure prominently in <u>Jonah</u>). This new art would be based not "on the idea of linear succession but on the idea of combination: the conjunction, the diffusion, the reunion of languages, spaces, and times." The key structural element would be the fragment which is "the form that best reflects the ever-changing reality that we live and are":

> The fragment is not so much a seed as a stray atom that can be defined only by situating it relative to other atoms: it is nothing more nor less than a <u>relation</u>.[50]

Tanner's work on the "fall-out from 68" involves a constant effort of conjugation, the establishing of relationships between stray atoms, through the interplay of the different levels of the discourse, the shifts from the indicative to the subjunctive mode, and the unexpected connections set up between the episodes.

The tensions developed by these strategies point to the central problem in dealing with Brecht's influence on Tanner. "Brechtian" cinema is normally associated with "montage," the use of editing to break down "the wholeness of reality" in order to construct a social discourse, and this approach is (as we shall see) not absent from Tanner's films. But their basic unit is the shot-sequence, which is more usually associated with a contemplative cinema based on a Bazinian respect for the integrity of time and space. Such a procedure has often been regarded as contrary to the analytic method encouraged by Brecht, but it can be justified in Brechtian terms, as suggested by Robert Stam in his account of the "subversive charm" of Jonah:

> A film like Jonah crystallizes and actualizes our desires even while it criticizes them. It follows the way pointed by Brecht: to dream, to tell stories, but at the same time to step out of the story and criticize it. Distancing is effective, after all, only if there is something such as an emotion or a desire to be distanced.[51]

This necessary tension between involvement and detachment is, as Stam points out, basic to Brechtian theater and can be related to the tension between realism and structuralism that underlies Tanner's development of Brechtian practice.

Tanner's strategy in using shot-sequences seems also to suggest a position close to that of Fredric Jameson, who argues that cultural developments have created a situation in which the Brechtian concept of estrangement needs to be turned against itself:

> ... when modernism and its accompanying techniques of 'estrangement' have become the dominant style whereby the consumer is reconciled with capitalism, the habit of fragmentation itself needs to be 'estranged' and corrected by a more totalizing way of viewing phenomena.[52]

The tension between fragmentation and relationship is reminiscent of Williams on "the struggle for relationships, of a whole kind," and Jameson's idea is supported by the paradox that Tanner creates estrangement by means of the shot-sequence, which is a privileged element in Bazin's polemic for "a more totalizing way of viewing phenomena." Tanner argues that "by not cutting within a sequence," he is able not only "to give back to a scene its reality" but also to create an "alienation effect" because of "the traditions in the eye of the spectator."[53]

These "traditions in the eye" derive from "the traditional narrative techniques brought to near perfection by Hollywood," which "form the appearance of reality by the destruction of real space and time within a sequence or scene by fast-paced and quick cutting." The techniques of classical realism thus create a perceptual structure which is "directly related to the ideological use of film in which the audience is led by the nose like a sleep-walker from the first scene to the last."[54] Although the spectator is led by the nose, it is the eye with which Tanner is concerned in his efforts to "break the chain." He objects that "the classical narrative codes" bring about "the effacement of all traces of work" by concealing the fact that "the camera is a heavy instrument, completely unlike the eye." To maintain the illusion, therefore, "it is the cutting which carries the burden of the 'look,' the restoration of the mobility of the eye."[55]

The illusion of continuity created by the cutting in the classical realist film is also designed to conceal the spatial limits of the frame. To Tanner "the frame is a completely arbitrary spatial definition, as arbitrary as the stage of the theatre" so that the "absence of cutting" creates a tension between respect for real space and a sense of theatrical artifice.[56] Tanner's style works to heighten this tension, beginning with Charles, in which, as he points out, "often the scene begins on the empty setting, and the character enters as in the theatre, and then goes out again."[57] The refusal to make things easy for the spectator's eye leads to the rejection of what Stam calls "the constant flow of identification via the ongoing exchange of glances by which conventional films plug us into the psychological and diegetic momentum of the story."[58] This breaking down of the classical structures of identification is the basis for the estrangement effect in Tanner's first two films, but in Return from Africa the camera itself becomes "an element of alienation." In classical realist films, camera movement, like the editing, is supposed to be "invisible" and so is always keyed to the movement of the characters; Tanner is thus able to challenge the "traditions in the eye" when "the camera moves for no apparent reason," with the result that "the alienation effect is doubled."[59]

Despite Tanner's rejection of the basic strategies of classical realism, he does acknowledge that his films do contain "certain elements dependent on the 'classical' code of representation: the effect of the real, recognisable characters, for example." But he insists that these elements function merely as "landmarks for the spectator," as a means of keeping the discourse within the circle, and that they operate only "within the 'fragments' of the film" and never "at the level of the global structure." Jonah, for example, includes "the realism of everyday life" and "characters that can be recognised (but not identified with)," but these familiar elements are estranged "in the final account" by "the constant distortion of the representational system" which the film plays with and dismantles even while it emanates from it.[60]

Tanner's aesthetic is, in fact, based on an acknowledgment of "the impossibility of really showing the reality" and a refusal to create the illusion that it can be and has been shown.[61] His approach thus becomes "a matter of decomposing reality rather than of reconstructing it," and his aim is to create a "realism of desire" that would be rooted not in illusion but in the need to establish a complex relationship with reality:

> It is the basis of my work on writing [écriture] and on fiction, this movement of coming-and-going, between the attraction of the real and disconnection from the real, between the 'true' and the 'false.'[62]

The effect of this shifting perspective is to give the films something of the quality of fables or parables. Berger has suggested that the parable is a means by which the artist tries to make "the relation between particular and universal fully explicit."[63] By this definition, Tanner's films are not fully fledged parables (since this relation is never fully explicit) but the tendency towards parable represents a break with the grounding of realism in the particular.

The break is not complete, however, since, as Todd Gitlin suggests, the films are "fables which begin with close observation of the material world" and their concern is with the politics of everyday life:

> It is inside daily life, in work and family, that freedom and desire are genuinely at issue....

In this most everyday of everyday-ness, everything is at stake.⁶⁴

It is part of the paradox of the parable that Gitlin's comment is not contradicted by Le Peron's insistence that "Tanner is not a film-maker of the 'lived,' of the transparency of everyday relationships." Le Peron points to a "kind of invisible thickness which sets things at a distance and which forbids all naturalisation," and it is this distance that allows Tanner to estrange the familiar structures of everyday life.⁶⁵

One of the key devices by which Tanner sets up this distance and breaks the continuity of realism is his use of quotations, sometimes (as in Charles) acknowledged, sometimes (as in Jonah) woven into the web of the discourse and delivered in a tone halfway between incantation and everyday speech rhythms. The effect of these quotations is suggested by Guy Debord's distinction between citation and displacement. Whereas citation involves fragments torn out of context and given a general and theoretical authority,

> displacement is the fluid language of anti-ideology. It appears within communication which knows that it cannot pretend to hold any guarantee in itself and definitively. It is, at its highest point, the language which cannot be confirmed by any ancient and supra-critical reference.⁶⁶

As in Brechtian theatre, the dialogue in Tanner's films often sounds like quotation even when it is not, and the effect is to work against any sense of a "natural" authority. These "voices" from outside add to other elements in the films which break down the linear structures of narrative so that, as Le Peron notes, although the characters may end up where they started, the films are not "defeatist" because the outcome of the fiction "corresponds only to the image" and is modified by (among other things) the subjunctive mode of the quotations.⁶⁷

The rejection of a "natural" authority does not imply for Tanner a rejection of nature. In response to humanist culture, which has tended to refer to natural causes to explain social conditions, socialist culture has tended to concentrate on social problems and to ignore natural phenomena. Many critics have found that this is a problem in Brecht, and the need to find a viable relationship between the social and natural dimensions of human experience has engaged a number of radical thinkers. We have already noted Williams' concern with "the struggle for relationships" on a social and personal level and Lefebvre's argument that the germs of future developments exist "in society as in nature." The problem is that, in isolating social from natural causes, socialism is acting as a distorting mirror of the processes of post-industrial capitalist societies. Berger points out that in these societies, "the sense of continuity once supplied by nature is now supplied by the means of communication and exchange--publicity, TV, newspapers...."[68] It is this unnatural continuity with which Tanner and Berger are concerned, and one way of challenging it is to compare it with the suppressed natural continuity. Thus, as Gitlin puts it, "in this Tanner-Berger vision, everything returns to its biological roots" and Jonah "intimates the need for a new politics--a politics rooted in love for the material world--whose actions cannot yet take place."[69]

In order to develop this vision, as we have seen, Tanner has to break with the ways of seeing that have presented themselves as "natural." He gets closer to nature by establishing a distance from it, thus preventing it from being used as an alibi for social inertia and testifying to the problem of representing nature through the dominant codes. Nowhere is this problem more apparent than in representations of sexuality and the human body. Paz argues that "contemporary art has not given us an image of the body" and that this function has been "turned over to couturiers and public-relations men."[70] Tanner's cinema bears witness to this problem through its combination of closeness and detachment. The use of shot-sequences stresses the physical and biological presence of bodies but the sexual act is never shown and nudity is only rarely presented. Since the act of sex cannot actually be shown except in pornographic films, Tanner argues that the filmmaker has to stop somewhere and might as well "stop before": "And in stopping before, one signifies, one marks, for the lack of anything better, the cultural corruption that rules in this domain."[71]

Despite the absence of titillating imagery, erotic tensions are important in Tanner's cinema and they relate to the tensions between realism (body) and structuralism (sign).

Paz defines eroticism as "an expression of the sign body," but adds that "the sign body is not independent; it is a relationship and it always has to do with the sign non-body, whether it is a movement toward it or away from it."[72] The issues raised by this relationship are discussed by Ferruccio Rossi-Landi, who distinguishes between idealistic semiotics, according to which "signs are not bodies just because all bodies are signs--what remains a body is of no interest," and materialistic semiotics, which accepts "that signs are also bodies, and that not all bodies are signs":

> That there are no signs without interpreters is a generally agreed upon statement. But the point is that the intervention of the interpreter, necessary as it is, does not suppress the materiality of bodies, nor does it transform into a sign what is not a sign.... Bodies are to be encountered both outside of signs and within signs themselves. Interpreters are bodies with needs, desires, illnesses, etc., and not only bodies capable of using signs. If you put a man into jail, what you put into jail is not only an interpreter, but a physical body as well. If you kill a man, you kill a man, and not only an interpreter.[73]

It is this tension between body and sign that distinguishes Brechtian from conventional theater. In the latter, the aim is to fuse the two so that each becomes the other's alibi, the actor's body disappearing into the sign/character but remaining sufficiently present to discourage the spectator from becoming aware of the character as sign. Brecht splits sign and body apart, making the spectator aware of the character as sign but also of the actor as body, thus promoting awareness of the structuring process and of its limits.

Tanner draws on Brecht to free the body from the false continuity created by "public-relations men" and the classical realist cinema, as well as to resist the twin dangers of seeing it simply as sign (structuralism) or non-sign (realism). And, as in Brecht, this strategy is accompanied by the use of humor to break down conditioned responses. Tanner has said that his aim in Charles was "to avoid being too serious ... it is a game in order not to be too edifying"; and Louis Marcorelles has commented on the film's debt to "the spirit of Free Cinema" because "its humour always compensates for the possible excess of gratuitous indignation."[74] However, Tanner later discovered problems with the effect of humor, similar to those he explores in relation to eroticism:

> I was very much surprised when I saw audiences in Paris and Geneva watching La Salamandre. They were laughing in the right places, but far too much, far too much. I realised the oral satisfaction they had when they picked up on those lines, and I didn't like it.... Irony is a kind of double-edged weapon; you can laugh at anything in the end, and it is also a sign of weakness.[75]

As a result of this experience, he downplayed the role of humor in Return from Africa and The Middle of the World, but he returned to it in Jonah, after which he again commented, "I'm beginning to mistrust humour, a double-edged weapon that can be turned against you."[76]

Tanner's uncertainty reflects the contamination of humor as an ideological weapon. His use of it has been seen as a sign of a lack of commitment, his rejection of it as a symptom of puritanism. Yet, once again, it is precisely the tension that becomes important in the films, and Tanner has clearly defined this tension in one interview:

> I'm aware of the dangers of humor, the dual nature of irony, but everyone works with contradictions, that's how things move forward. I like to create situations where that contradiction is built-in.... This is something I've learned from Brecht --to say something serious in a funny situation, or the other way around, creates a tension for the viewer.[77]

Tanner's attitude is effectively summed up by Stam in a comment on Jonah: "The film ... shows that work can be frivolous and play serious.... Art, meanwhile, is both work and play."[78] This blurring of the boundaries between work and play is held in delicate suspension in Jonah, but the strength of the underlying tensions is revealed in Messidor, which deals with two young women whose energies can find no outlet in work or play. As Tanner puts it, their journey through Switzerland becomes "a game between them ... and a game against everything else," and this game has both destructive and creative elements, since "on the one hand they completely disintegrate and, on the other, they find themselves."[79]

The stakes at play in Messidor are much higher than those in the relatively straightforward "game" strategy in Charles, although even in this first film tensions do stem from the realization that "madness is revolutionary freedom confined to the self." The confinement of Charles in an asylum and of the young women inside the Swiss border represents the confinement of human desire within the structures of ideology, a confinement which Tanner's cinema brings to consciousness and contests. Tanner's strategy of remaining within the circle but on the margin creates a cinema which can both express the need for continuity and break down the false continuity that hides real fragmentation.

NOTES

1. André Bazin, quoted in J. Dudley Andrew, The Major Film Theories (London: Oxford University Press, 1976), p. 161. The passage is from the first French edition of Bazin's Orson Welles (1950) but is omitted from the revised edition of 1972 on which the English translation is based; see Andrew, André Bazin (New York: Oxford University Press, 1978), p. 242n.

2. Octavio Paz, Conjunctions and Disjunctions, trans. Helen R. Lane (New York: Viking Press, 1974), p. 40.

3. Louis Althusser, Lenin and Philosophy and Other Essays, trans. Ben Brewster (London: New Left Books, 1971), p. 201.

4. Henri Lefebvre, L'ideologie structuraliste (Paris: Editions Anthropos, 1971), p. 162; Yves Velan, "Barthes," in John K. Simon, ed., Modern French Criticism (Chicago: University of Chicago Press, 1972), p. 320n.

5. Edward L. Said, "Abecedarium Culturae: Structuralism, Absence, Writing," in Simon, pp. 378-9.

6. E. P. Thompson, The Poverty of Theory and Other Essays (New York: Monthly Review Press, 1978), p. 98.

7. Sylvia Harvey, May '68 and Film Culture (London: British Film Institute, 1978), p. 95.

8. Michael Tarantino, "Alain Tanner: After Jonah," Sight and Sound, Winter 1978/79, p. 42.

9. Bertolt Brecht, "Against Georg Lukacs," in Ernst Bloch, Georg Lukacs, Bertolt Brecht, Walter Benjamin, Theodor Adorno, Aesthetics and Politics (London: New Left Books, 1977), p. 85.

10. "Entretien avec Alain Tanner," Cahiers du cinéma, 273, January-February 1977, p. 38.

11. "Alain Tanner: Charles mort ou vif," Cahiers du cinéma, 213, June 1969, p. 30.

12. "Entretien," p. 39.

13. "Tanner: Charles," p. 28.

14. Linda Greene, John Hess, and Robin Lakes, "Subversive Charm Indeed!" Jump Cut, 15, p. 9.

15. "Entretien," p. 38.

16. Raymond Williams, Keywords (Glasgow: Fontana, 1976), p. 257.

17. Raymond Williams, The Long Revolution (London: Chatto and Windus, 1961), p. 287.

18. Williams, The Long Revolution, p. 288.

19. Raymond Williams, Politics and Letters (London: New Left Books, 1979), p. 218.

20. John Berger, About Looking (New York: Pantheon

Circle and Margin / 51

Books, 1980), p. 56; Berger, The Moment of Cubism and Other Essays (New York: Pantheon Books, 1969), p. 32.

21. Todd Gitlin, "Jonah Who Will Be 25 in the Year 2000," Film Quarterly, Spring 1977, p. 37; Robert Stam, "The Subversive Charm of Alain Tanner," Jump Cut, 15, p. 7.

22. Lefebvre, p. 162.

23. Serge Le Peron, "Ici ou ailleurs," Cahiers du cinéma, 273, January-February 1977, p. 45.

24. Max Ernst, Zurich Surrealism Catalogue (1934), quoted in Uwe M. Scheede, René Magritte: Life and Work, trans. W. Walter Jaffe (Woodbury, N.Y.: Barron's, 1982), p. 38.

25. Theodor Adorno, Looking Back on Surrealism (1956), quoted in Scheede, p. 125; Berger, About Looking, p. 158.

26. Scheede, p. 38.

27. Richard Appignanesi, "The Screenwriter as Collaborator: An Interview with John Berger," Cineaste, vol. 10, no. 3, Summer 1980, p. 15.

28. Appignanesi, p. 15; Berger's text in A Fortunate Man is juxtaposed with images by Swiss photographer, Jean Mohr, as also in A Seventh Man (1975).

29. Appignanesi, p. 18.

30. Appignanesi, p. 19.

31. Jill Forbes, "Interview with Alain Tanner," Films and Filming, February 1982, p. 21; Appignanesi, p. 16.

32. Forbes, p. 21.

33. Appignanesi, p. 16.

34. Berger, The Moment of Cubism, p. 4.

35. George Szanto, "Oppositional Way-Signs: Some Processes Within John Berger's History-Making, History-Unravelling Experiment," College English, vol. 40, no. 4, December 1978, p. 372.

36. John Berger, Pig Earth (London: Writers and Readers, 1979), p. 6.

37. Berger, The Moment of Cubism, pp. 21-22.

38. Berger, Cubism, pp. 16-20.

39. John Berger, The Success and Failure of Picasso (New York: Pantheon Books, 1980, originally published 1965), pp. 59-60.

40. Roland Barthes, "The Structuralist Activity," in Critical Essays, trans. Richard Howard (Evanston: Northwestern University Press, 1972), pp. 214-5.

41. John Berger and Jean Mohr, A Fortunate Man (London: Writers and Readers, 1976, originally published 1967), pp. 101-2.

42. Szanto, pp. 371-2.

43. Szanto, p. 364.

44. Michael Tarantino, "Tanner and Berger: The Voice Off-Screen," Film Quarterly, Winter 1979-80, pp. 35, 39, 41-2.

45. Szanto, p. 373.

46. Tarantino, "Tanner and Berger," pp. 41, 38.

47. "Tanner: Charles," p. 29.

48. Brecht, quoted by Hans Ego Holthusen, "Brecht's Dramatic Theory," in Peter Demetz, ed., Brecht (Englewood Cliffs, N.J.: Prentice-Hall, 1962), p. 108; the passage is taken from "Notes to Die Rundkopfe und die Spitzkopfe" but is omitted from the translation in John Willett, ed., Brecht on Theatre (New York: Hill and Wang, 1964).

49. "Entretien," p. 41.

50. Octavio Paz, Alternating Current, trans. Helen R. Lane (New York: Viking Press, 1973), pp. 21, Foreword.

51. Stam, p. 7.

52. Fredric Jameson, "Reflections in Conclusion," in Bloch et al., Aesthetics and Politics, p. 211.

53. Lenny Rubenstein, "Alain Tanner: Isolation and Ennui," Film, July 1975, pp. 16-17.

54. Rubenstein, p. 16.

55. "Entretien," p. 40.

56. "Entretien," p. 40.

57. "Tanner: Charles," p. 29.

58. Stam, p. 7.

59. Rubenstein, pp. 16-17.

60. "Entretien," p. 39.

61. Tarantino, "Tanner: after Jonah," p. 43.

62. "Entretien," p. 39.

63. Berger, Pig Earth, p. 195.

64. Gitlin, pp. 36-7.

65. Le Peron, p. 47.

66. Guy Debord, Society of the Spectacle (Detroit: Black & Red, 1970), #208.

67. Le Peron, p. 47.

68. Berger, About Looking, pp. 189-90.

69. Gitlin, pp. 39-40.

70. Paz, Conjunctions, p. 125.

71. "Entretien," p. 41.

72. Paz, Conjunctions, p. 115.

73. Ferruccio Rossi-Landi, "Signs and Bodies," in Seymour Chatman, Umberto Eco, Jean-Marie Klinkenberg, eds., A Semiotic Landscape/Panorama sémiotique (The Hague: Mouton, 1979), pp. 357-9.

74. "Tanner: Charles," p. 29; Louis Marcorelles, in André Pâquet, ed., Jeune Cinéma Suisse (Montreal: La Bibliothèque nationale du Québec, 1970), p. 4.

75. Rubenstein, p. 17.

76. "Entretien," p. 41.

77. Lenny Rubenstein, "Keeping Hope for Radical Change Alive: An Interview with Alain Tanner," Cineaste, vol. 7, no. 4, p. 24.

78. Stam, p. 6.

79. Tarantino, "Tanner: After Jonah," pp. 40-1.

3: CHARLES DEAD OR ALIVE

It is that we are told we are free, and that we are shaping our common destiny; yet, with varying force, many of us break through to the conviction that the pattern of public activity has, in the end, very little to do with our private desires. Indeed the main modern force of the distinction between 'the individual' and 'society' springs from this feeling.
--Raymond Williams[1]

Capital can only exist as such if it continually reproduces itself; its present reality is dependent upon its future fulfillment. This is the metaphysic of capital.
--John Berger[2]

Near the middle of Tanner's first feature film, there is a sequence which helps to define the formal strategies and social perspective introduced here and developed in the later films. Charles Dé, the fifty-year-old owner of a watch factory in Geneva, has abandoned his family and his business and fallen in with a young couple, Paul and Adeline, who live outside the city. As Charles is driving them to their home, they stop at an area of waste land on the outskirts of the city to perform a "ritual." Paul and Adeline always stop at this place to gaze at the landscape; it is, however, completely devoid of the picturesque elements usually associated with the aesthetic appreciation of nature. They admire the suburbs and satellite towns but dislike Geneva because it is full of American spies, banks, and tourists. Adeline describes a "beautiful" dream she has had in which Geneva was turned into a coaling port and its parks into a magnificent steel-works. Her rapturous vision exposes the way in which the cleanliness and tidiness on which Geneva, the capital of international bureaucracy, prides itself is made possible only by the concealment of the industrial labor on which its wealth depends.

The visual appearance of the city is just one of the masks by which an advanced capitalist society conceals its actual workings. As we have seen, Tanner's own attitude to Geneva makes explicit what is implied by Adeline's dream:

> I have a personal disgust at Geneva; I am truly horrified by this city of parks, of international institutions, where there are above all no factories, above all no workers, this city where above all we must not walk on the grass.[3]

The elimination of the signs of work combined with rigid social control is exactly what Tanner also finds in the "invisible" editing which is basic to "the classical narrative codes." This kind of editing functions "to efface all traces of the work" involved in making a film.[4] Tanner's basic strategy is thus to make visible the social processes of concealment.

This strategy is introduced immediately in the pre-credits sequence of Charles Dead or Alive. The camera pulls back from a close-up of a young worker, hesitantly praising his employers, to reveal that he is reading from a text and being filmed by a film crew working on (as we will soon discover) a television documentary. This revelation of "another" camera within the fiction alerts us to the unseen presence of Tanner's own camera and thus to the whole process of constructing the fiction which we are seeing. In addition, we quickly realize that the worker's words are not his own, but his speech is being documented as a "real" event by the television crew. As the reporter will later confirm, their cinéma vérité approach precludes any awareness of their own complicity in the construction of the fiction of the ceremony which they are filming or of their contribution to the unease which leads to the worker's clumsiness. The tensions set up in this first sequence by the spoken text and the presence of the television camera anticipate the various levels of discourse which will collide with each other in the course of the film. We also see the first signs of Charles's discontent--as he retires to the washroom during the ceremony in his honor--so that his crisis of consciousness is linked to the pressures created by the official discourses which Tanner's cinematic strategies call into question.

By continually disrupting the habitual ways of thinking and seeing developed and exploited by the conventional cinema, the film makes us aware of the work that has gone into its own production but also of the work that we must do to complete its meaning. We are prevented from placing Charles's behavior in ready-made categories, and our own effort to make sense of his situation parallels his attempt to come to terms with his personal experience in its social context. At the level of verbal discourse, for example, we have to assimilate a wide variety of idioms, including colloquial speech, inner monologue, television interview, radio newscast, recitation, quotation, and song. The cues by which we recognize the appropriateness of the idiom to the situation are often either deferred (as in the case of the worker's speech) or absent (as when the cynical detective sings of the pleasures of May while tailing Charles's daughter, Marianne, through the snow). Visually the film creates disorientation by the use of long takes coupled with unexpected cuts which link sequences without respect for temporal or narrative continuity. This approach reaches an extreme during Charles's stay with Paul and Adeline, when he alternates between feelings of freedom and frustration. After he has drunkenly denounced Paul in a bar for his complacency, there is a sudden cut to a brief sequence in which the two men happily walk down a country road with Adeline between them.

Although the dislocations at this point in the film can be related to Charles's state of mind, the film's strategies do not allow us to identify its vision with that of the protagonist. The relationship that the film sets up between the spectator and its images has been well described by André Cornand, who calls Charles "one of the most Brechtian works of our age":

> Tanner, while soliciting a certain sympathy for his characters, facilitating a desire to project ourselves on to them, succeeds at all times in maintaining the spectator at the critical distance necessary to allow reflection and to provoke an intellectual response.[5]

58 / A Possible Cinema

The basis of Tanner's style is to be found in this tension between sympathy and detachment. As we will see, the problem of establishing a satisfying relationship to reality is one with which Charles is deeply concerned, but the spectator also has to deal with the problem of the film's relationship to reality.

The depiction of Charles is loosely based on the actual experience of the country doctor who was the subject of Tanner's prize-winning television documentary (in which he used <u>cinéma vérité</u> methods). Tanner has himself compared his own program to the one in <u>Charles</u> and has described the effect of its making on its subject:

> ... there was the arrival of television in this man's life and the fact that he considered himself in certain respects a bit like the spokesman for the medical profession. We stayed with him for two weeks and he spoke to us at great length. This brought about a sort of breakdown in his life, and the making of the program affected him very deeply. Afterwards he had a rather serious nervous depression.[6]

Charles undergoes a similar crisis as a result of his participation in the television program, and the film places this crisis within the context of the split described by Williams between "public activity" and "private desires." Television defines public and private spaces: it has an unsettling personal effect on Charles but this does not interfere with its public effect of helping to maintain things as they are.

The problem of relating "private desires" to social institutions suggests the terms in which the film responds to the events of May 1968. Although Charles's age and position would seem to separate him from the spirit of May, Tanner makes the connection explicit in a note to the screenplay: "The desires of his youth rise to the surface, but he can no longer make use of them."[7] Philippe Haudiquet describes <u>Charles</u> as "a child of the month of May," but May itself is referred to only obliquely in the film: in the detective's song and in Marianne's quotations and her activities in the student protest movement (her name, like those of the eight "Ma" characters in <u>Jonah</u>, also suggests that she is a child of May).[8] This oblique approach indicates that

Charles, despite its roots in actual events, presents itself not as a direct reflection of reality but as a "fable." Tanner points out that "it is certain that no Swiss industrialist left his factory like the hero of my film," and Haudiquet argues that the recourse to fable is "a ruse ... to return to reality and to bring it home to the spectators."[9]

The fable-like quality of the film accounts for the playful aspect of much of its imagery, but there is one element of this that can be easily missed by non-Swiss spectators. A note to the screenplay indicates that the action is set "in a near future" and, although there is no explicit statement to this effect in the film itself (which is sub-titled "little historical fresco"), there are a few indications that it is, in effect, post-dated. The opening ceremony is in celebration of the one-hundredth anniversary of the founding of the firm by Charles's grandfather after the collapse of the anarchist commune in the Jura mountains of which he had been a member. Not all Swiss spectators might be aware that this chronology would set the action in the late seventies but they would be alerted to the film's play with time by the radio newscast, towards the end, which reports the result of a referendum in which a narrow majority has voted in favor of giving women the right to vote. Swiss women did not, in fact, win voting rights until 1971, and the effect of the newscast is to project the action into a possible "near future." The news report is heard in the background while Charles, Paul, Adeline, and Marianne are preparing a meal, and they completely ignore it. In fact, Marianne turns the radio off, without comment, while the announcer is describing the response of politicians to the result. The spectator is thus left to decipher the meaning of the non-response of the characters to a hypothetical event which relates to actual political and social attitudes.

The elements of "play" and "fable" work against the creation of an illusion of reality which can be simply consumed. Even the title plays with generic conventions by arousing expectations of a film about an outlaw. Inasmuch as he does move from the center to the margins of society and is tracked down by a detective, Charles does become an outlaw. But before he begins this movement (the reverse of his grandfather's), the title has come to seem more like a question that Charles addresses to himself as he takes stock of the compromises on which his life has been based.

In the first half of the film, Charles is often seen studying his face in mirrors, as he does in the opening sequence when he withdraws from the public ceremony to the privacy of the washroom (the film's title is superimposed on the mirror after Charles has left). When Charles later looks into a mirror, he sees himself as being split vertically in two between his physical reality and his public image, between the left side (with his heart) that is rotting and the other side which makes "an honest living" (his self-justification during the abortive interview that follows the ceremony). Rehearsing before a mirror for the second interview and then watching his image on the television screen, Charles comes to see better and no longer needs the spectacles which have been sold to him so that he will see less clearly. He breaks both with the image that has been imposed on him and with the limited vision of "reality" which that image implies.

The unsettling effect of the mirrors on Charles can be related to the spectator's experience of the uncertain "reality" of Tanner's films. Serge Le Peron describes this experience in terms of a "a mirror in which one is simultaneously there and not there, in a space that is both real and unreal; there where appearances are at home and, with a disturbing strangeness, confess themselves as such."[10] Once the mirror-image is seen as an image it can make visible the hidden processes that have shaped what is accepted as reality. The problem is that as a young man, Charles needed a sense of reality against which to define himself, and that the "reality" offered by his family tradition has proved to be illusory. During the long interview in which he defines his dilemma, he describes the pressures that forced him to follow his father as head of the family firm. He recognizes that his opposition to his father was based on a vague "adolescent dream" and admits that his new responsibilities gave him a "feeling of existing, of doing something." This feeling has gradually disappeared, so that he has had to search for something else outside his work and has come to the point at which he finds it difficult to believe in his own existence. He now sees what he "instinctively repressed" in his youth: that the family tradition in which he reluctantly put his trust is a "structure" in which he has been trapped.

Just as awareness of this structure surfaces during the interview, so the oppression under which Charles suffers begins to become visible. He has been unable to resist the pull towards the center of the social system in which the self is defined entirely in material and conventional terms. When, after his disappearance, Charles's description is broadcast on the radio, he can be described only by the clothes he was wearing and by his unconventional behavior (he is not his normal self). The problem is compounded by the genuine difficulty of knowing what is going on inside another person. Charles's son, Pierre, can only view his father's crisis as bad "publicity" for the firm and wonders what is going on in his head. He resolves this problem, created by his own lack of imagination, by labeling his father as a madman. It is the difficulty of seeing the sources of oppression that leads Charles to doubt his own existence. As he stares into his bathroom mirror, he recognizes that oppression cannot be read on his face as it could be if he were black or a "guest-worker" from the south. Later, in a drunken monologue, he extends this new awareness to cover the whole of his society, in which "oppression no longer has need of a face, still less of guns" because "its ignoble order is inside ourselves."

After witnessing Charles doubt his own existence on the television screen, a man at the bar looks questioningly at the actual Charles sitting next to him. Does this look imply a simpler world to which Charles has no access? Does it conceal similar doubts on the part of the looker? Bourgeois society is able to brush aside the implications of this uncertainty by converting it into a problem of appearance and reality: the detective does not hesitate to offer a sexual explanation of the mystery created by Charles's behavior, and Pierre sends his father to a mental hospital for readjustment to the "real" world. But it is precisely the reality of this world that is being called into question. For Pierre, his father's existence is simply a matter of legal signatures: either Charles is sane and will thus take responsibility for his son's "improvements," or his refusal to do so will confirm his insanity and render his signature (and his existence) unnecessary. By assigning motives, the establishment posits the presence of an authentic self beneath the "mask" of physical existence, but since these motives are already defined and evaluated by the established vision of the world, any failure to conform to this vision must be regarded as abnormal. A speech at a public ceremony can be accepted as an expression of "reality" despite the evident oppression that determines its format; a social challenge can be dismissed as a sexual transgression; and the equation of the "real" and the "normal" can be maintained by the brainwashing performed first by the publicity machine and then, if all else fails, by the psychiatrist.

As Charles suggests, it is difficult to fight this system which presents itself as "human nature" and lacks visible signs by which it can be identified. It is associated in the film with the phrase "like that" (comme ça), which suggests its fixed and pervasive quality. During the interview, Charles describes how his hopes for change in the post-war years were countered by his father's belief that "nothing ever changes" because "the world is made like that, once and for all." From this point of view, the family tradition is part of a natural or metaphysical hierarchy which descends from God to the world, to "just and eternal" Switzerland, and finally to the Dé family. Belief in this order meant that Charles's father could always act as if he were right and always was right "if one accepted his definition of the universe." The pressures on Charles to conform to this vision led him to accept the status quo, and he later admits to Paul that he did not pay his workers well because "things are like that." Charles can no longer accept the family tradition nor the view of the world and of Switzerland on which it is based. In his drunken monologue, just before his denunciation of faceless oppression, he insists that his father's beliefs have been replaced by a new "certainty that our mountains are not the bearers of any truth or any virtue." Yet, although this value-system has collapsed as a lived reality, it still persists as an insidious ideological force. The complicity of the television program within the system, despite the supposed neutrality of the cinéma vérité approach, is revealed by its title: "People Are Like That."

Marianne objects to this title on the grounds that "people are never 'like that'." The title promotes the idea of a fixed human nature, uninfluenced by history and environment, and works against an awareness that, even in the most "transparent" of documentaries, our responses are influenced by the role-playing of the subjects and the preconceptions of the filmmakers. The worker's uneasiness during his speech shows how the presence of the camera can affect what is filmed, and the interviewer admits that

that he had already decided on the theme of "the business spirit of a family" before he first approached Charles. The interviewer seems sincere in his concern to capture reality using <u>cinéma vérité</u> techniques, but the ease with which this approach can be absorbed into the system is revealed by Pierre's complaint that the failure of the first interview has cost the firm a chance for free publicity. When Charles does try to express his anxieties in the second interview, Pierre can only think of the harm done to the firm's image. Our response to the revelations made by Charles during this interview is complicated by the way in which the television cameraman moves in and out of frame as Charles and the interviewer walk across the lawn, and then by the shift from the process of making the program to its transmission. We have to come to terms not only with the ideological pressures which Charles is describing but also with the implications of these pressures for the process by which his experiences are being represented. A technique which sets out to duplicate reality is seen to be inadequate, and Charles's search for an effective response to a society based on consumption is paralleled by the film's search for a language that cannot be accommodated by the dominant vision.

Despite its title and the limitations of its technique, the television program does help Charles to confront his situation. It exposes the contradiction between the family spirit on which bourgeois society is supposedly based and the actual growth of large corporations. The worker declares in his speech that the workers at the Dé factory do not feel like "anonymous employees" but see themselves as "members of a family." The pressures put on the worker as he makes this speech may be compared with those put on Charles to enter the family business, and Charles comes to appreciate anonymity when he hides out in a hotel under a false name. Although he has sacrificed his own desires to the needs of the family, he has had to struggle to preserve the "family" firm against the pressures to expand which have now been accepted by his son. During the first interview, he agrees with the interviewer's formulation that he had tried to retain "a certain personality ... the personality of your family," as opposed to "the anonymity of a large concern." He becomes increasingly irritated, however, with this complacent view of his situation, and the interview breaks off with his bitter denunciation of the materialism masked by the ideal of the family: "I have a villa, a family, a dog, numerous insurance policies, two cars, a chalet in the mountains with a Swiss flag in the garden." Yet he is forced to acknowledge that the signs of his problem are not always visible, admitting that "there is no flag, but it is as if there was one."

Against the fixed and timeless definition of the family spirit provided by his father, Charles develops a historical account of his family tradition. His grandfather started the firm after the failure of the anarchist movement to transform society, and thus a family business based on the principles of mechanical order (watch-making) has its roots in a political movement dedicated to the freedom of the individual. Charles says that his grandfather "died of sadness," but the enterprise he founded moved rapidly through the expansionary evolution of capitalism: from craft workshop through the age of the machine to the verge of the computer era. During the first interview, Charles explains that his grandfather was a craftsman, his father a combination of craftsman and business man, while his son is only a business man. As the interviewer points out, Charles sees himself as marginal to this process, despite his efforts to maintain something of the human element inherent in the craft stage. He has been unable to cope with the reality of the structure set up by his grandfather and is stifling in the materialistic expansion of the "security" in search of which the defeated anarchist fled to Geneva.

Charles's rebellion against the material comforts by which he is surrounded is expressed most fully in his attitude to the car. As he mentions in the interviews, he owns two cars and escapes from his everyday reality by going for drives on Sundays. The first sign of his decision to break with this reality occurs when, after having watched himself on television, he gets into his car, sits silently for a while, and then (instead of driving home) leaves it to go to a hotel. Later in the film, the car will be closely identified with the establishment, through the figure of the detective who never leaves his car unless he has to, and through Marianne's Self-Defense League which attacks the system by disrupting traffic. During the ceremony in the waste land, Charles delivers a lecture in which he explains why he dislikes cars: 1) the driving position is unhealthy; 2) traffic has become the dramatic art of idiots since accidents become tragedies and taking risks on the highway is all that is left

of adventure; 3) cars create a system of accumulation in
which people never meet; and 4) the oil and sheet-metal
companies control and destroy the cities while persuading
people that their desires are being satisfied. This lecture,
delivered in a self-mocking tone, is borrowed from Henri
Lefebvre, whose work Charles will be seen reading later in
the film, but it is Paul who translates words into action by
pushing Charles's car over the side of a ravine.[11] Even
here the film insists on a complex response, since Paul himself owns a car and has earlier complained of Charles's
treatment of his car. Nevertheless, the immediate result
of the destruction of the car is a feeling of release as the
trio walk happily along the road and Charles carelessly
throws away the car keys which Paul hands to him.

The function of the car in modern society is just one
example of the dependence of the establishment (summed up
in the figures of the business executive, the detective, the
lawyer, and the psychiatrist) on what Marianne calls "a
permanent aggression." Since people are continually being
told that they have everything, to be unhappy is to be abnormal. As Charles is being taken to the clinic at the end
of the film, he quotes Lefebvre to the ambulance men:

> Saint Just said that the concept of happiness was
> new to France and to the world in general; the same
> could be said of the concept of unhappiness, for
> to be aware of being unhappy presupposes that
> something else is possible, a different condition
> from the unhappy one. Perhaps today the conflict
> 'happiness-unhappiness' or 'awareness of a pos-
> sible happiness-awareness of an actual unhappiness'
> has replaced the classical concept of Fate. And
> this may be the secret of our general malaise.[12]

The ambulance men respond to this pronouncement by turn-
ing on the siren to drown out Charles's disturbing voice
and so that they can drive through red lights. It would
seem that the "permanent aggression" has triumphed with all
the inevitability of "the classical concept of Fate." Yet the
process by which Charles is finally eliminated has revealed
(by exposing the contradictions within bourgeois ideology)
the possibility of another outcome, just as the film has shown
the role of the media in this ideological aggression but also
demonstrated possible ways of combating it.

After the ambulance carrying Charles has disappeared into the concrete whiteness of the city, which seems like a gigantic asylum, we are left with the ambiguity of the final caption: "He who laughs last laughs longest." This can be taken as a sardonic acknowledgment of the triumph of the establishment, but it seems more like a challenge and a threat. The closing images offer little immediate hope, but the final effect can be related to one of the quotations that Marianne prepares for Paul: "It is only through those without hope that hope can be restored to us. (Walter Benjamin)." Only on the level of the narrative is the outcome bleak and desolate, and the film is as subversive in its use of narrative codes as it is in its account of the society in whose cinema narrative is the dominant level. Just as Charles does not present a transparent reflection of reality, so the ending refuses to resolve the film's tensions by allowing the spectators to "feel it is finished, completed at the end, so that when they leave the cinema, the film is one thing, while the rest of their lives is an entirely separate matter."[13] The spectators cannot remain secure in their relationship to the film and are drawn into an awareness that Charles's final incarceration merely makes explicit and visible the condition that he was in before his rebellion.

The film suggests that the modern media--the dominant narrative cinema, the popular magazines of which Marianne speaks, the cinéma vérité documentary--actively transmit or passively reflect the image of happiness based on consumption. The exposure of the actual unhappiness masked by this image is the first step towards the development of possible alternatives. Two such alternatives are represented by Paul and Adeline's withdrawal to the margins of society and by Marianne's active intervention. Paul and Adeline allow Charles to share their retreat from the pressures of the system, but they are themselves a bundle of contradictions. This in itself makes them a welcome relief from the monolithic structure of bourgeois society (which carefully conceals its contradictions), but it also renders them impotent in relation to that society. Paul's non-conformism is undercut by his liking for cars, his reluctant acknowledgment that as a sign-painter he is an artist who runs a "small business," his initial aggressiveness towards Marianne, and his acceptance of Adeline in the role of housewife despite his proud assertion to Charles that they are not legally married. His offer of Adeline to satisfy Charles's presumed sexual needs sums up his radicalism in its parallel with the detective's assumption that Charles must be involved in a ménage à trois. Without denying Paul its sympathy, the film confirms Charles's drunken denunciation of him as "a dirty little bourgeois who is playing at freedom." Charles yells that nothing will be resolved until Paul learns to see the present "with the eyes of the future" and is willing to "start from an absolute demand." Earlier Charles has said that Paul suffers from the Swiss national vice of "a rather immoderate taste for mediocrity," and his marginality is seen as a form of neutrality similar to that professed by the Swiss establishment.

Tanner himself has referred to the tragedy of the marginal couple in Charles who deprive themselves of all possibility of "a true political engagement or of finding other forms of contestation."[14] They believe that they have cut themselves off completely from society but they are still dependent on their car, on the nearness of a doctor when Paul cuts his hand, and on the money he earns as a signpainter. Paul responds to Charles's admission that his workers were not well paid by expressing his own fear of having paid employees. This refusal of the complications created by economic responsibilities echoes the vague aspirations of the young Charles and contrasts with the practical independence of Marianne. She is first seen walking determinedly between high-rise buildings and then begging for money from her father. Her admission of her economic dependence and her analysis of the way in which society uses the need for money to force students to conform, coupled with the fact that she is the only member of the family to respond to Charles's human needs, point to an engaged detachment like that towards which the film as a whole is working. Her attitude allows her to expose the workings of the system as well as the weakness of Paul's isolation from it. When Paul accuses the Self-Defense League of actually being the aggressors, she delivers a lecture on society's aggressiveness while she confronts Paul, who stands in an aggressive posture with his sledgehammer on his shoulder.

It is Marianne who introduces the quotations into the film as a cure for Paul's taste for mediocrity. She gives him a maxim for every day which he has to learn by heart and then relate to "what is happening." These maxims are taken from radical thinkers, from the graffiti of May, and from popular wisdom. Their defiance of logical and conventional categories--"Be realistic. Ask for the impossible. (Anonymous)"--creates the sense of a strong undercurrent opposed to the "common sense" used to support the social order. The use of quotations also relates the political struggle to the problem of language. Even before Marianne has introduced her maxims, we have been exposed to the worker's speech, which, in effect, quotes the language of his employers. We have also listened to Cilette, a young neighbor of Paul and Adeline, recite a poem that she has had to learn for school; unexpectedly, this poem deals with the frustrations of living in Switzerland, where words are "wasted like water." Charles even quotes himself in front of the bathroom mirror and complains that his words rot in his throat and upset his stomach. The prevalence of quotation further undermines the idea of film (or television) as a transparent medium which can simply record "natural" or spontaneous behavior. Marianne's project merely recognizes the element of quotation already present in social relationships, but she freely acknowledges her sources and finds value not in the automatic repetition of the quoted texts but in the contradictions that emerge from the collision between the cryptic quotations and received opinion.

One example of this collision is the challenge to sentimental idealization of the family in "We can't all be orphans. (Jules Renard)." This quotation relates to the role of family tradition in Charles's life and is introduced immediately after Paul has told Charles that he and Adeline are not married. It suggests the futility of a complete rupture with one's social context even if it is seen as narrow and oppressive. The failure of conventional values and language is illustrated in the opening ceremony, and Paul has responded to this failure by trying to cut himself off from convention and ceremony (although, as we have seen, he and Adeline have their own private rituals). Charles finds a sense of release in Paul's retreat, but as the friends relax in a rare moment of satisfaction after their feast, Charles argues that "a certain ceremonial is a sign of consciousness of what one is doing." His claim that this was once the function of the "festival" points once more to his debt to Lefebvre, who argues that "the advent of competitive capitalism" led to the "decline of Style and the Festival." The feast itself is an example of what Lefebvre calls the survival of the festive spirit in "meetings, parties and funfairs that are a poor substitute and fall short of the required glamour" but are "none the less pleasant enough imitations on a reduced scale." From this perspective, Charles can be seen as a contribution to Lefebvre's "revolutionary plan to recreate a style, resurrect the Festival and gather together culture's scattered fragments for a transfiguration of everyday life."[15]

Charles cites the examples of children to whom even peeing can become a ceremony and of the behavior of crowds at football matches. Paul accuses Charles of unnecessarily complicating existence, but this exchange on ceremony is central to an understanding of Tanner's strategies in all his films. "Life likes us to be conscious of it," insists one of Marianne's quotations (from René Char), and Tanner's discourse, with its use of quotation, fable, dislocation, and surprise, works to make us conscious of our social and cultural environments. This consciousness works against the ability of the establishment to accommodate the political movements opposed to it. To quote Lefebvre for one final time, "alienation is spreading and becoming so powerful that it obliterates all trace or consciousness of alienation."[16] Charles shows Tanner working towards a style that will challenge his audience to become fully conscious of social (and cinematic) processes, a style that creates a dialectical tension between anarchy and ceremony and that rejects both dogma and neutrality.

NOTES

1. Raymond Williams, The Long Revolution (London: Chatto and Windus, 1961), p. 88.

2. John Berger, Pig Earth (London: Writers and Readers, 1979), p. 213.

3. "Alain Tanner: Charles mort ou vif," Cahiers du cinéma, 213, June 1969, p. 30.

4. "Entretien avec Alain Tanner," Cahiers du cinéma, 273, January-February 1977, p. 40.

5. André Cornand, quoted in the edition of the screenplay published in L'Avant-scène du cinéma, 108, p. 39.

6. "Tanner: Charles," p. 29.

7. Tanner, L'Avant-scène, p. 10; the reference to the date of the action discussed in the next paragraph is on the same page.

8. Philippe Haudiquet, "Un enfant du mois du mai," L'Avant-scène, pp. 8-9.

9. Haudiquet, pp. 8-9.

10. Serge Le Peron, "Ici et ailleurs," Cahiers du cinéma, 273, January-February 1977, p. 45.

11. See Henri Lefebvre, Everyday Life in the Modern World, trans. Sacha Rabinovitch (London: Allen Lane, 1971), pp. 100-1.

12. Lefebvre, p. 206.

13. Lenny Rubenstein, "Alain Tanner: Isolation and Ennui," Film, July 1975, p. 16.

14. "Tanner: Charles," p. 30.

15. Lefebvre, pp. 36, 38.

16. Lefebvre, p. 94.

4: THE SALAMANDER

> Objectivity in the ordinary sense of the word--
> total impersonality of observation--is all too ob-
> viously an illusion. But <u>freedom</u> of observation
> should be possible, and yet it is not. At every
> moment, a continuous fringe of culture (psychol-
> ogy, ethics, metaphysics, etc.) is added to things,
> giving them a less alien aspect, one that is more
> comprehensible, more reassuring.
> --Alain Robbe-Grillet[1]

> Discourses are not once and for all subservient to
> power or raised up against it, any more than si-
> lences are. We must make allowance for the com-
> plex and unstable process whereby discourse can
> be both an instrument and an effect of power, but
> also a hindrance, a stumbling-block, a point of
> resistance and a starting point for an opposing
> strategy.
> --Michael Foucault[2]

Like <u>Charles Dead or Alive</u>, The Salamander starts from a narrative premise that could have provided the basis for a detective film: did Rosemonde really shoot her uncle, as he claims, or did he injure himself while cleaning his gun, as she insists? As in <u>Charles</u>, this initial enigma is quickly replaced by more important questions about society and language. Pierre, a journalist, is forced by his economic situation to accept a commission from Swiss television to write a screenplay which will reveal the "truth" behind Rosemonde's story. The project would seem to be one that could expose the social aggression with which <u>Charles</u> was concerned, but Pierre ultimately fails to fulfill the commission because of the difficulty of comprehending Rosemonde's experience and because he is unable to find a language by which the experience could be adequately articulated.

Pierre does come to realize that the "crime" of which Rosemonde is accused is not an isolated event but an expression of social tensions which call into question conventional attitudes to "reality." Tanner suggests this broader context in his notes to the screenplay:

> Rosemonde ... is someone who is physically incapable of adapting to the conditions of everyday work.... Whereas her uncle represents, in a schematic way, the traditional myths which frame reality.[3]

As a marginal intellectual, Pierre rejects these myths but is unable to find an alternative to the established structures. The film tries to go beyond his failure by incorporating it as one of several shifting perspectives which implicate the spectator in the process of stripping away "the traditional myths." There is a double focus: Rosemonde's struggle to cope with the pressures of her society and the search for a language in which this struggle can be expressed without being falsified or neutralized.

As often in Tanner's films, the problem of point of view is introduced in a pre-credits sequence. In this case, we are shown the shooting of the uncle but in such a way that we cannot see who pulls the trigger. The graininess of the images and the jerky hand-held camera movements suggest that this is newsreel footage, and the use of slow-motion evokes attempts to use such footage to discover the killer after certain assassinations. But the camera is so close to the action that the crucial details cannot be made out; in fact, it is not until later that we realize that this sequence contains an incident which may be an accident or attempted murder. All that can be grasped at first viewing is the threat of violence in the presentation of a gun as the opening image, an element of mystery related to this violence, and the relation of this mystery to the final pan up from the face of an old man in obvious pain to the passive face of a young woman.

Then, from a point of view that is too close for comfort, we are shifted abruptly to a long shot of the same young woman walking briskly beside a river. After the unsettling effect of jerky movements, the camera now tracks smoothly along with the subject in a way that creates a feel-

The Salamander / 73

ing of release (to be confirmed by later uses of the same movement), but we are now too far away to make any judgments about the feelings of this woman, of whom we know so little. The shift from closeness to detachment raises the problem of finding an adequate perspective but also makes us aware of the influence of the film's strategies on our response to this problem. Our consciousness of the medium is then heightened by the superimposition of the credits over Rosemonde's walk by the river and by the description of the film as a "chronicle in black and white colours."

These first two sequences are wordless, but in the sequences following the credits we are plunged into the world of intellectuals, which is dominated by words. Pierre is first seen on the telephone to Paris, having trouble getting through to a man called Louis Roy. This device quickly establishes the problem of verbal communication, Pierre's ties to French culture (with Roy's name suggesting its continued imperialism), and his concern to write an article on Brazil in order to extend his political and personal horizons. Pierre then discusses his economic difficulties at the kitchen table with a woman friend, an actress who is trying to learn her lines, while a bearded man is silently marking essays. He is thus defined as an intellectual existing on the margins of society. But this marginal group lives comfortably within the circumference of the social circle and Pierre is able to fall back on a commission to write a screenplay for another friend. Pierre initially sees this project as an unpleasant necessity imposed on him by his material needs, and his idea of employing yet another friend (Paul) as collaborator is motivated by his desire to buy time to work on his more important article on Brazil. As Return from Africa will make clear, Swiss society is one in which time is money, and it is within this context that Pierre's attempts at sociological journalism must be evaluated.

Pierre's approach is based on respect for the facts, on a painstaking gathering of material which can then be organized into a statement which will presumably elucidate the mystery and challenge the point of view of the establishment. But this method takes little account of the contradictions within his own personality. In his notes to the screenplay, Tanner comments that Pierre's "existence is rather disordered on the material level" but that he attempts to counter this disorder by a precise and ordered approach to life.[4] Rosemonde will disrupt this precarious order, as when she pays a badly-timed visit while he is trying to write his article on Brazil and proceeds to seduce him. She violates his attempts to keep things in their proper places: he insists on keeping gloves in the glove compartment of his car and expresses surprise when she wants to eat at four in the afternoon.

Along with Pierre's desire for an ordered life goes a caution which is revealed when he puts his hand out of his window to test for rain even though it is quite visibly not raining. This image, too, seems to suggest a distaste for the outside world which contradicts his theoretical emphasis on fieldwork. When he and Paul take Rosemonde to visit her family in the country, Pierre is deeply depressed outside in the cold but finds that "everything is perfect" when next seen perched on a radiator in his hotel room. Rather than explore Rosemonde's childhood environment with Paul, he prefers to imagine the warmth of Rio and goes back into the hotel saying that he is returning to Brazil (foreshadowing the imaginary and indoor journey to Africa in Tanner's next film). The tension in his character between retreat and research leads to an unpredictability which reaches a climax when he marches through a forest with Paul chanting, "how near is happiness! ... how far away is happiness!" This oscillation between hope and despair is common in Tanner's characters and illustrates the difficulty of establishing a fixed and permanent outlook in a world of violent contradictions.

Pierre's lack of stability is especially obvious because he has adopted a policy of neutrality in dealing with the outside world, a peaceful co-existence which allows him to accept work from the system without endorsing its values. The weakness of this strategy is exposed by its failure to cope with the specific case of Rosemonde, and its political implications are hinted at early in the film when Paul's boss tells him that he is wanted on the telephone by Nixon or Brezhnev (he can't remember which). As we suspect, the caller is Pierre, and the joke here anticipates the idea of "normalization" developed in The Middle of the World.

Pierre's reluctance to separate himself from a world which he distrusts and which threatens to accommodate him is contrasted with Paul's attempt to create his own environ-

ment in which he can be free from the compromises to which
Pierre has to submit, as well as from the drudgery that
wears Rosemonde down. As a writer, he refuses to accept
commissions which do not interest him and supports himself
by working as a house-painter (suggesting a parallel with
his namesake, the sign-painter, in Charles); as a worker,
he refuses to be tied to his job and goes off to write whenever he feels the urge. Tanner describes Paul's life as a
balancing act:

> Materially, and to some extent also spiritually, Paul
> walks every day on the edge of the abyss but without bitterness and according to a precise choice
> which serves the goals that he has set for himself.[5]

These goals involve living in the country with his wife and
daughter, and he is thus able to place the emphasis on the
"retreat" side of the dichotomy with which Pierre struggles.
But he too is faced with a contradiction in the collapse of
his aesthetic detachment when confronted with the reality of
Rosemonde.

Pierre expresses scorn for Paul's "petite famille,"
which flourishes "in the middle of the most complete spiritual misery," but the order of this strange household does
survive all threats from outside. When Paul confesses to
Lydie (his wife) that he has slept with Zoé, the typist employed by Pierre and Paul (which may or may not be true
but, in any case, comes as something of a surprise since
he was last seen massaging Rosemonde and is now performing a similar operation on his motorcycle), she responds by
commenting on how complicated his life has become and proceeds to recite from a text by Heine. Their relationship
seems to thrive on their abstraction and isolation, a quality
that he tries to apply to his writing by refusing to meet
Rosemonde and by transforming her into the ficitonal Héliodore. But Paul is finally able to come closer than Pierre
to Rosemonde, perhaps because he shares her lack of education, and the presence of his daughter does imply some
hope for the future, if he can avoid the pitfalls inherent in
trying to combine marginality with the "petite famille." In
reply to Pierre's scorn, he sees conceiving a child as "the
great law of nature" which promotes consciousness by restricting his freedom and making him aware of the burden

of daily life (repeating the emphasis in <u>Charles</u> on the need
for a reality to define oneself against). The Heine text
quoted by his wife is a vision of a new generation conceived
in "freely chosen embraces, not in the bed of duty," which
will achieve "free thoughts and feelings." The failure of
this vision to become reality since Heine wrote it in 1828 reflects the resistance of the established order, but the hope,
tenuously, remains.

To the consciousness which he gains by balancing his
freedom with the demands of reality, Paul adds a respect
for ceremony which relates him to Charles Dé. He is able
to turn everyday acts, like taking off his coat and sweater,
into small ceremonies which give form to his life but which
prevent these actions from becoming merely routine. His
habit of bursting into song when he feels sad typifies the
way in which his behavior blends the ceremonial and the
spontaneous to subvert conventional responses. When he
takes a long and formal leave of his wife before going to
visit Pierre in Geneva, the absurdity of the ceremony does
express the stability of this relationship that constantly defies the "normal." Our response to this image is, however,
complicated by the structure of the opening sequences,
which have introduced Rosemonde, Pierre, and Paul but not
allowed us time to settle into conventional attitudes towards
them nor established a secure perspective from which to
view them.

Such a perspective seems to be forthcoming with the
introduction of an apparently omniscient off-screen voice
over shots of Paul's journey on his motorcycle through the
country to the city. The voice tells us that Paul lives in
the country for economic rather than romantic reasons, that
his house is close to the French border, that despite appearances he is a writer, not a house-painter nor a singer,
and that today is October 25 (the commentary will continue
sporadically to date the aciton until its completion on December 20). But the security apparently offered by this omniscient perspective is undercut by the explicitness with
which it provides information that would conventionally be
worked into the narrative action. The voice is female, and
thus lacks the "authoritative" quality associated with the
male commentator in the documentary tradition (even in the
Free Cinema movement). Nor is it anchored in the perspective of a character within the fiction. As Michael Tarantino

puts it, the commentary provides "factual information that is parallel, rather than perpendicular, to the film's narrative."⁶ Its uncertain status means that it cannot clarify our relationship to the film and can only add to the complexity of the points of view with which we have to deal.

The claim of the commentator to see behind appearances and to establish time and place allies her to the narrative stance developed in the conventional novel and taken over by the conventional cinema. She does admit, however, that her insight is limited by the Swiss border, since France is "a country where one never knows what is going to happen from one year--or even one month--to the next." Despite the predictability of Swiss life, her own attitude is so unpredictable that it becomes increasingly difficult to evaluate her tone. Sometimes she seems to speak for the establishment, as when she describes a strike by the foreign garbage-workers as a savage threat to "order and exterior cleanliness." She describes the valley in the Juras where Rosemonde's family lives as "a very beautiful valley," only to be contradicted immediately by Rosemonde's outburst at "this filthy valley."

The commentator's identification with the official viewpoint is not complete, however, since she can conclude Pierre and Paul's subversive musings in the forest by informing us that "a silent majority is composed of people like you and me," who are easily misled by the divisive forces of a so-called democratic society. In general, her interventions are obtrusive and redundant: she announces that night has fallen while Rosemonde has waited for Pierre to finish his typing, only to have Pierre immediately remark that "night has fallen"; she corrects the mistaken impression of Rosemonde's mother that Paul is an educated man, thus depriving Paul of the opportunity of doing so himself. She describes what Paul writes in his notebook during his wanderings in the valley and what Pierre thinks in the warmth of his hotel room, but she is unable to resolve any of the mysteries of the film--even the detective mystery with which it begins. Yet she does have the last word, as she describes the schizophrenic behavior of Christmas shoppers, and that last word is "normal."

Despite the uncertain tone of her interventions, the viewpoint of the commentator is theoretically based on the equation of reality with normality, and it is the collision between the calm assurance of her voice and the quiet desperation of the images that provides a basis for the search for a perspective that will not betray reality. The omniscient viewpoint depends on the belief that reality can be known and that, once misleading appearances have been stripped away, this reality is unproblematic. It is their inability to agree on such a perspective that sparks the debate between Pierre and Paul during their first session together and that explicitly raises the question of how reality can be known. Paul bases his fictional approach on a virtuoso performance in which he "explains" Rosemonde simply by reference to her name. The apparent magic here turns out to be a process of deduction (worthy of the policeman that he insists he is not) grounded in the predictability of social conventions, in this case the habit of rural Catholic families of naming their children after the saint on whose name day they were born. Most of Paul's suppositions are later confirmed (in almost the same words) by Rosemonde's uncle, and his device of naming his heroine Héliodore is explained by Rosemonde's later comment that if she had been born six days later she would have been called Héliodore. But Paul's exploitation of social conventions, he discovers, really explains little about Rosemonde, and his fiction collapses when overwhelmed by her actual presence.

Even before Rosemonde's eruption into their lives, Pierre undercuts Paul's performance by insisting that there is "one small problem," namely where to find "reality" in his story. He insists that the woman and her uncle both exist and that he is concerned with "reality," with "things." Paul does come to accept that the "facts" have decided against their completing the assignment, but these facts have equally undermined Pierre's contribution to the project. The difficulties that Pierre has in coping with a reality closer to home than Brazil are foreshadowed by the images that he has pinned to his wall along with press clippings on Rosemonde's story. We see, among others, a glossy photograph of a young couple, a poster bearing the legend "The Police and You," and a deodorant advertisement. This collage of political and publicity material exposes the ideology of the bourgeois state, but it also reveals the naïveté of Pierre's belief that reality is made up of facts that have merely to be collected and consumed. Reality resists such an approach, as is shown when Pierre tries to take photographs of Rosemonde but enters enthusiastically into the game as she plays the role of a model. She quickly tires of this and Pierre is able to photograph her customary blank stare (and include these images in his collage), but the sequence reveals how "publicity" (pose, disguise, deceit) can take on the appearance of reality. Of course, the pose may reveal more of reality than what it is meant to conceal, but the problem of meaning (and how it is affected by the medium) still remains. Pierre himself seems rather uncomfortable with the aggressiveness of this image-taking, as he suggests when he points out that his camera is "less dangerous than a gun."

The problem is stated in Paul's distinction between the journalist who repeats what he has learned and the writer who tries to discover the meaning of what he already knows. The difficulty of this latter endeavor in a world of advanced technology is already apparent, and Pierre seems to realize this as he sits thinking at his hotel window in the Jura valley. According to the commentator, he has discovered a meaning in the parallel between "the crushing of bodies, out there" (Brazil? the Third World?) and "the crushing of spirits, here." But this "meaning" has no purpose since, even if it is known and spoken, it will be "swept along like a pebble in the great grey river of information." Neither Pierre nor Paul are able to save their story from the flood. Pierre's journalistic objectivity disappears when Rosemonde seduces him, but he never succeeds in getting very close to her. When she fears that she will be accused of robbery, he can only suggest that she leave for Paris, which, as Paul points out, is a suggestion that makes more sense for himself than for her. The journalist cannot sufficiently efface himself to respond to Rosemonde's reality, but Paul can use his imaginary creations to help her gain an insight into her own situation and provide her with a practical approach to her problems. His first sight of her in Pierre's bed leads to the abandonment of his fiction because she is not as he imagined her, but they do establish a relationship of mutual respect. He massages her back to ease her tensions, walks joyfully down a country road with her while discussing her education and his sexual preferences (as far as we know, they do not become lovers), and takes her on a long streetcar ride during which he is able to help her discover some of the political implications of her situation.[7]

Although it is Paul whose approach proves flexible enough to arrive at an understanding of reality that will allow some political intervention, it is through Pierre's journalistic inquiries that we first learn about Rosemonde. His first attempts run into difficulties, as the commentator puts it, "because of the very personality of Rosemonde," but these difficulties tell us more about the society in which she must survive than they do about her personality. Her ex-landlady describes the "dreadful disorder" of her room and her former employer complains of her inability to arrive on time. On finding Rosemonde's apartment in the suburbs, Pierre unquestioningly assumes that Suzanne, her roommate, is his quarry, a trivial mistake but one that (coupled with his earlier failure to remember her name) suggests his remoteness from the task at hand. Nevertheless a certain bond between them does develop in the early stages of his research. As he drives her home from her job in a sausage factory, they share their disgust at a system which uses the promise of a pension to keep people at their jobs and to prevent them from realizing their desires while they are still young. The commentator also describes Pierre's approval of Rosemonde's decision to give up dressmaking because she did not like the job. But it is clear that his sympathy extends mainly to those areas of Rosemonde's existence which parallel his own as a marginal intellectual. Her background makes it more difficult for her than for him to cope with the pressures of a society that does not regard dislike as a good reason for leaving a job. As they discuss the problem of pensions, Pierre's irony cannot disguise the temptation that the ordered life holds for him, but Rosemonde has to face up to the full consequences of an order based on repression.

Initially Pierre's investigations may seem more likely to unmask this order than Paul's fictional speculations. Yet the contrast between their methods of approaching Rosemonde provokes a complex and double-edged irony. Pierre's interview with Rosemonde is intercut with images of Paul writing about Héliodore in his country retreat. Pierre's engagement with reality is contrasted with the romantic isolation of Paul, who is seen alone through the frame of a window and who gains inspiration from playing the piano. Yet this isolation does not totally undermine his project. After the commentator describes Pierre's approval of Rosemonde's quitting her job, there is a cut from

Rosemonde silently chewing gum to Paul writing (as the commentator informs us) of Héliodore's distaste for the petty restrictions to which workers have to submit. Imaginatively Paul has grasped the basis of Rosemonde's problem and is able to verbalize her emotional response. A few moments later, Rosemonde tells Pierre that people think she is not normal; there is a cut to Paul composing a passage in which Héliodore realizes that her desires are normal and that the abnormal must be looked for elsewhere. He seems to be able to draw significance from the raw facts with which Pierre is still working, even to the point of expressing Rosemonde's unrealized inner thoughts, but the question with which we are faced (and which he will face when he meets her) is whether his ability with words does not falsify the reality of someone who has been deprived of all "voice" in her existence.

Rosemonde's reality has already been presented in such a way as to call into question any intellectual or verbal response. A shot of Rosemonde working silently and mechanically at the sausage factory is cut into the sequence in which Pierre and Paul discuss their different approaches. The wordiness of the intellectuals is contrasted with the oppressive silence imposed on the workers by the mind-numbing nature of their jobs and the noise of the machines. The insertion of Rosemonde's silent presence reveals the actual conditions with which the theoretical discussion must come to terms. The obsessive rhythms made necessary by the sausage-stuffing machine expose the constraints imposed on her, but the sexual overtones of her actions as she fills the sausage skins create a tension with the deadening routine and suggest (in a debased form) the vitality which allows her to fight back. Her life is defined by a rhythm of constriction and release in which her energies are pushed towards violence. She tells Pierre that when she leaves the factory she always experiences a desire to cry out or break something. When she finally quits her job after a confrontation with the foreman, her feeling of release is given a sexual connotation by the image of the sausage meat spilling from the unattended machine. It is also conveyed by the lateral tracking shot which follows her as she joyfully crosses a bridge over the Rhone and by a shot of her floating in the swimming pool. The pool has sexual connotations because of its association with Roger, her boyfriend, and it is also a confined version of Tanner's frequent use of water to suggest a natural freedom (as when Rosemonde describes her brief idyllic escape to the sea and when Paul walks beside the river in the country with his daughter).

Rosemonde clearly possesses a natural force which society tries to suppress, but which emerges at the end of the film when she breaks through social conventions by caressing the legs of customers at the shoe store where she now works. Her behavior can be taken as confirmation of Pierre's final assessment that she is a "whore" (although she ridicules a male customer who takes her caress for a sexual advance), as a sign of madness (the view of her bosses), or as an act of guerrilla theater (she is, after all, only parodying the owners' belief in the need for sex appeal to sell shoes). When she is dismissed, she subverts the concern of the owners to hush the matter up by taking her leave with exaggerated politeness, but very loudly. Her vitality cannot be accommodated into the system which has driven her to the point that her refusal to suppress her desires must cut her off from the "normal" world. The link between her "madness" and that of Charles Dé is suggested by the fact that one of the anonymous customers whose legs she caresses is played by François Simon, who had played the role of Charles.[8] His brief presence is a reminder of the extent and power of the social forces that drive those who refuse to conform to behavior that can be conveniently dismissed as "mad."

The process by which Rosemonde is alienated from her social context has already led to her rejection of her Catholic upbringing and of her uncle's combination of authoritarianism, patriotism, and militarism. She continues to wear a cross around her neck but uses the Pill and, as the commentator observes when she is with Roger at the pool, she is "ready to be damned." The tension between religious background and sexual needs relates Rosemonde's situation to Henri Lefebvre's argument that "basic repressions," supported by religious traditions, prevent "man's <u>adaptation to his desire</u>" and force sexuality to seek "an outlet in new forms of religiosity."[9] According to Lefebvre, the "foremost" of these repressions is "the ideological relation of fecundation to the sexual act," and Rosemonde's current sexual behavior needs to be related to the fact that she has had an illegitimate child. Here the "natural

law" by which Paul justifies his "small family" creates a
contradiction, since Rosemonde both fulfills its demands
(by having a child) and transgresses (by not being married) the social codes which base their authority on it.
Rosemonde says that she wanted to keep her child, despite the practical difficulties involved, but her mother has
taken it from her because "one more or less" will make little difference to this large family. The contradictions running through social and sexual codes are evident in the
mother's gesture because Paul has already suggested, and
the uncle confirmed, that Rosemonde was sent to live with
her uncle so that there would be "one less mouth in the
house." In this respect, Paul's use of the social and sexual predictability of the Catholic world-view to "explain"
Rosemonde becomes an act of collaboration with the forces
that oppress her. These forces may initially derive from
her rural background but their continuity with the ideology
of modern urbanized Switzerland is suggested by a sequence
in which Pierre listens to mass on a transistor radio while
Paul sits reading a newspaper called "La Suisse."

Rosemonde tries to combat the dominant ideology
through her sexuality but also through a counter-culture
which apparently subverts established values. She has a
poster of the Beatles on her wall, and she plays the juke
box and drinks Coca-Cola when Pierre takes her to a café.
Yet her obsessive shaking of her head to loud music is
itself seen as a compulsion created by a society which
gives any vitality a demonic quality. The screenplay describes her as "a little like an African dancer who is trying to enter into a trance to exorcise his demons."[10]
These demons are related to cultural violence by a cut
from her obsessive silent shaking after Suzanne has turned
off the music, to her stillness amid the noise of the factory.
As she talks to Pierre, Rosemonde links her desire to dress
as she wants with her awareness that she is "not very normal." To be normal in this society is to be willing to wear
a disguise; Rosemonde resists but has no effective cultural
resources to support her resistance. She attacks the narrow social order through the disorder of her personal life,
her sexual freedom, her primitive rituals, but the mass
culture to which she gravitates offers no real means of
exorcising the fear and guilt on which bourgeois society
(and thus mass culture) depends.

As a woman and as a worker, Rosemonde has a very limited space allotted to her by society. One of Marianne's maxims in <u>Charles</u> insists that "there are no foolish people, only foolish jobs"; after quitting the sausage factory, Rosemonde reads newspaper advertisements but only finds jobs that offer her no challenge or for which she is not qualified. She does not know what a computer programmer is but feels sure the job is not for her. Society, which claims to provide a framework for individual freedom, pushes her back within herself until she is left sitting naked on her bed and contemplating her situation in an impotent inner monologue. "People detest my independence," she says, "and always try to break me." But despite her impotence, she also seems to be the salamander of which Paul writes in his notebook, a poisonous animal that can pass through flames without being burned. This description is not specifically applied to Rosemonde, but Paul (according to the commentator) does write it during his explorations in the valley where she was brought up. The final sequence, in which Rosemonde smiles amid the crowd of Christmas shoppers, leaves us in some doubt as to whether she has passed through the flames unscathed. Michel Euvrard argues that her smile indicates a madness which is "the other side of the collective schizophrenia" and that "thrown into the fire again, this time the salamander burns"; but he acknowledges another response which sees the smile as a sign of happiness based on the new consciousness that she has gained from her discussions with Paul.[11] The openness of the film requires that the spectator, like Pierre and Paul, resolve the uncertainties generated by Rosemonde's character in terms of his or her own situation.

The ending, in fact, can be seen as a return to the beginning, with Pierre preparing to leave for Paris, Paul whitewashing the same wall, and Rosemonde as enigmatic as ever. There is also a return to the slow-motion and absence of words of the opening sequences. Yet this circularity, and the failure of Pierre and Paul to find a way to express Rosemonde's experience, is countered by the progressive unmasking of the political pressures associated with life in "neutral," capitalist Switzerland. Aggression is introduced by the opening image of a gun pointed at the audience, and this gun is later identified with Swiss militarism by the uncle who sees it as a symbol of "our liberties." He keeps his gun on the wall next to the telephone, and Rosemonde later says that she shot him because he made her do useless work, "like in the army." The contrast between the uncle's libertarian ideals and the actual slavery that he imposes on his niece reproduces the contradiction between ideology and reality in Swiss society. Social aggressiveness is exemplified by the foreman in the sausage factory, by the youth who assaults Rosemonde in her village, and by the police inspector who investigates the robbery at the shoe store. And it is this aggression which provokes the violence that is seen as criminal in Rosemonde, as shown in her account of the shooting and in her toying with a knife when the foreman talks down to her in the factory. She feels that everyone wants her to be something other than she is, and her protest in the shoe store represents her rejection of the aggression of the "normal."

Pierre and Paul see themselves as opposed to this aggression but their methods are dangerously similar to those of society. Paul objects to Pierre that the journalist functions like a policeman, while Pierre compares Paul's explorations in the valley to the movements of Indians creeping up on their victims. Later, in desperation, they work together for the first time and dominate Rosemonde threateningly as they question her. Her response is to dramatize herself by acting out an obsession with their shoes, and then to deflate them by comparing them to Laurel and Hardy. Rosemonde thus eludes their investigation by a protective role-playing, which she may also adopt in the affair of the theft at the shoe store. Rosemonde claims not to have seen Roger for a week before the robbery, but we see him steal her keys while she is sleeping and are shown a close-up of the white tennis shoes that he puts on. Later, when Paul buys a similar pair of tennis shoes, the owner comments that he is the second customer to buy a pair and to leave wearing them even though it is the height of winter. Because the shot of Roger lacing on his shoes is immediately followed by one of Rosemonde being interrogated by the police, the question of her role in the robbery is actively raised and the mystery of the shooting is replaced by another detective enigma.

Yet this new enigma is as irrelevant to the real concern of the film as the old one has become, especially once Rosemonde has confessed to shooting her uncle. There is no need to regard this confession as "objectively true," just as we cannot know why Pierre lies to Rosemonde when he tells her that he has not yet visited her uncle, or why Paul confesses to an affair with Zoé. The difficulty of separating fiction from reality, already embodied in the different approaches of Pierre and Paul, is incorporated into our experience of the film and has to be taken into account in responding to the social problems with which it is concerned. During the journey that Paul and Rosemonde take to the shoe store on the morning after the robbery, the importance of the shooting is seen not in deciding whether or not Rosemonde is guilty but in finding a response to its social significance as a real or imagined event. Paul explains that his fictional heroine shot her uncle because society had systematically prevented her from living "in her own skin," and he uses the fiction to help Rosemonde identify her true friends and real enemies. Rosemonde has earlier told him how her brother broke windows to rebel against their father; now he teaches her the difference between "breaking a window and breaking a window." She must learn not to break windows on her own but to see her experience as part of a collective cultural deprivation. He shows her that her bosses are among her enemies but also persuades her to return to her job. His ability to juxtapose Héliodore and Rosemonde, fiction and reality, at least temporarily allows him to give practical advice which recognizes the contradictions hidden by the monolithic structure of a system which grounds itself on a "natural" order of reality and normality from which any deviation is seen as criminal and/or insane.

The Salamander insists that these social problems cannot be divorced from the aesthetic problem of point of view. Both the documentary and the fictional approach are seen to involve the danger of accommodation to the dominant point of view, as is the omniscient perspective of the commentator. At one point, Pierre and Paul feel that they must start again from zero in trying to rescue their project, and Paul suggests that "a narrative in the first person" might be the answer. This suggestion is immediately followed by the sequence in which we see Rosemonde sitting naked on her bed and hear her "inner voice." Paul's hopes for the first-person approach are not borne out in this single sequence in which we have a privileged access to Rosemonde's mind: since the approach is limited by the consciousness of the subject, it can only provide a static view of her situation, especially now that she has been driven back into herself. The failure of this development signals the abandonment of their project by Pierre and Paul, but the brief adoption of the first-person mode does add to the number of perspectives that Tanner's film juxtaposes in order to make us aware of the "screens" that alienate us from "reality," and which established conventions try to hide. The conventions governing point of view are exposed as the aesthetic extension of the ideology defining social relations.

As Godelieve Mercken-Spaas has pointed out, Pierre, Paul and Rosemonde are all "misfits in society, literally confined to its edges."[12] They are marginalized by what Pierre denounces in the forest as "capitalism, in its fundamental perversity, and bureaucracy, in its obtuse dogmatism." But at least they are aware of their position, whereas ideology works to suppress consciousness of social and personal boundaries by creating the illusion that the subject is "the middle of the world." Rosemonde's performance in the shoe store exposes the existence of social and sexual boundaries, while Swiss chauvinism is attacked in an improvised piece of guerrilla theater on a streetcar in which Paul sings an Arab song while Pierre delivers a loud diatribe against foreigners. The bureaucratic obtuseness that underlies the social system is depicted in the visits to Pierre's apartment by an inspector from the Moral Defense division of the department of Civil Defense, and by a landlord's agent who has to estimate the value of the contents of the apartment in case they have to be seized in lieu of rent.

Since the action is not conveyed by a firm linear development of plot and character, such sequences do not demand that we adopt a pre-established point of view towards the issues raised but rather work to undercut all pre-established versions of the "truth." The film not only concludes, as Thomas Elsaesser suggests, that "reality is a complex and relative affair, to be approached only by way of possibly self-defeating bridges thrust into the unknown," but also insists that awareness of this complexity is the only basis for any political intervention in the social reality that oppresses Rosemonde.[13] Mercken-Spaas agrees that "the film systematically and defiantly brings out the ambiguity of knowledge" but her suggestion that "paradoxically, fiction decodes reality better than tangible evidence"

88 / A Possible Cinema

unnecessarily resolves one element of this ambiguity.[14] An awareness of the tensions between "fiction" and "evidence," on which The Salamander insists, may reduce the risk of the bridges being "self-defeating," as they are for Pierre and (perhaps) for Paul. In any case, our response cannot be that of the citizens of Geneva, who react neutrally but sympathetically to Pierre's xenophobic outburst but become hostile when told that it was only a "game."

NOTES

1. Alain Robbe-Grillet, For a New Novel, trans. Richard Howard (New York: Grove Press, 1965), p. 18.

2. Michel Foucault, The History of Sexuality, vol. 1, trans. Robert Hurley (New York: Vintage Books, 1980), pp. 100-1.

3. Alain Tanner, in the edition of the screenplay published in L'Avant-scène du cinéma, 125, May 1972, p. 7.

4. L'Avant-scène, p. 8.

5. L'Avant-scène, p. 8.

6. Michael Tarantino, "Tanner and Berger: The Voice Off-Screen," Film Quarterly, Winter 1979-80, p. 40.

7. Ernest Callenbach ("The Salamander," Film Quarterly, Winter 1972/3, p. 20) casually notes that Rosemonde "soon sleeps with Paul too," but this interpretation depends on assumptions about her character which the film is concerned to dispel.

8. The iconic force of Charles Dé in Switzerland is also seen in his reappearance (played by a different actor) in Patricia Moraz's The Indians Are Still Far Away (1977), in which he gives advice. to another young woman crushed by her environment.

9. Henri Lefebvre, Everyday Life in the Modern World, trans. Sacha Rabinovitch (London: Allen Lane, 1971), p. 84.

10. L'Avant-scène, p. 19.
11. Michel Euvrard, "La Salamandre," Cinéma Québec, vol. 1, no. 10, July/August 1972, p. 37.
12. Godelieve Mercken-Spaas, "Narrative Levels in Alain Tanner's La Salamándre," Film Studies Annual, 1977, Part One, p. 97.
13. Thomas Elsaesser, "The Cinema of Irony," Monogram, 5, p. 1.
14. Mercken-Spaas, p. 93.

5: RETURN FROM AFRICA

> The true exile ... is committed to waiting: when his society changes, then he can come home, but the actual process of change is one in which he is not involved.
>
> --Raymond Williams[1]

> Geneva--perhaps more exclusively than any other town in Europe--is a capital of words: words written in reports and on cheques: spoken words, interpreted and recorded.
>
> --John Berger[2]

Return from Africa opens with a slow tracking shot across the faces of a cinema audience absorbed in a film which, judging by the sound-track, is one of violent action: we hear the screech of brakes and a woman's voice (in English) complaining that she is being hurt. This aural violence emphasizes the passiveness of the spectators which is, however, at least partly an inevitable aspect of the experience of viewing a film. The image is an uncomfortable reflection of our own situation, but it also points forward to Aimé Césaire's description, later quoted by Vincent, of "this crowd which doesn't know how to crowd."[3] Our discomfort stems from the tension between community and isolation involved in watching a film, and thus we become aware that our experience of this film parallels both Césaire's frustration with the passiveness of his people and the problems of Vincent and Françoise in trying to find a satisfying social context. The link between the violent film and the passive response also relates aggressive film techniques to the colonial oppression which degrades Césaire's crowd and which Vincent and Françoise find in disguised form in Geneva. Since the violent film merely takes advantage of the fixed situation of all cinema audiences (including our own), this opening underlines Tanner's concern to work for change within the social context and the necessary limitations of human experience. He does not turn the violence of bourgeois society and its cinema against itself (as Godard does in Weekend) but creates an almost completely non-violent film in which supposedly cathartic violence is replaced by a movement towards a consciousness of the violence inherent in our social structures.

The second shot of Return from Africa shows the group of people who were absorbed in the violent film trying to come to terms with their experience by discussing it in a bar. Yet their apparently intense experience is immediately dissipated in words since they can think of little to say of the film other than that it was "not bad." The effect of their inarticulacy and their overlapping voices is intensified by the way in which the camera pans, apparently arbitrarily, back and forth across the group; but from this cacophony emerges the (male) voice of a commentator who proceeds to lay bare the strategies of Tanner's film. He tells us that it will be a black-and-white film, made up of words and about words, and that the poet quoted will be Aimé Césaire. This announcement also contains a brief discussion of words which can be "an act in themselves or a substitute for action," a means of self-discovery or self-escape. The introduction of the commentator exposes the way in which the film imposes order on reality and relates this process to the tension between words and action (or more fundamentally to the problem of language). This will not be an action film, or even a film of words, but a film on the gulf between the two and on the difficulty of performing meaningful actions in a world full of meaningless words.

It is this world that dominates the first section of the film, in which the frustration of Vincent and Françoise leads to their decision to work in a Third-World country. As he drives through the city on his return from work, Vincent recites the familiar street names and performs the routine function of changing gears at the usual places. He feels stultified by the lack of challenge in his life and his inability to influence the forces that control his society. His job working for a landscape gardener is relatively pleasant and satisfies the Swiss desire to create order in nature. It means, however, that he works for the privileged few who can afford large gardens and that he must

92 / A Possible Cinema

please a boss for whom "time is money." His boss cheerfully equates "business" with "cheating" and believes that this is a natural state of affairs ("that's life"), contemptuously pointing out that there is no cheating in communist countries. The hypocrisy of this social order is exposed by Vincent when he disconcerts a rich lady by taking at face value the false humility with which she asks if the workers would like tea. They treat her as if she were a maid, and it is her maid who returns with the tea. However, even the maid prefers the shelter of the garden to Vincent's joking suggestion that she come with him to Africa, which, she says, is full of snakes.

While Vincent's job entails the neutralization of nature, Françoise works in a gallery in which art is similarly neutralized. When she arrives at the gallery in the morning, a close-up shows her unlocking the door; later she is shown standing alone in the gallery; in the evening she is shown locking up again. The works of art in the gallery are modern (a Giacometti sculpture, for example) and their debt to primitive art suggests a critical attitude towards western culture. But this criticism has been deprived of any real effect by the treatment of art as merchandise and property. Capitalist society converts all values into material terms, as Vincent claims when he sings about politicians and merchants lining up behind big money, to the tune of the cathedral bells. Art and religion have been "accommodated" into the consumer society.

The cathedral is first introduced in the credits sequence, which consists of a slow pan across the Geneva cityscape. After moving across modern high-rise buildings and construction sites, the camera passes the cathedral, which stands out against the horizon, and then performs a loop before coming to rest on the cathedral as the music of Bach swells up on the sound-track. Although the cathedral is not seen again in the film, Vincent and Françoise evidently live close to it in the old part of the city and its bells become a kind of mocking chorus during their confinement to their apartment. The cathedral and the music of Bach point to a cultural tradition which the evolution of society has rendered increasingly irrelevant, just as the "family tradition of enterprise" in <u>Charles</u> has become a moribund ideal in the face of international corporate reality. The building in which Vincent and Françoise live has been condemned to make way for new development and they are its last tenants; the reality of their society is more honestly represented by the new apartment block to which they move, surrounded by the waste land of a construction site and dominated not by the sound of bells but by the noise of low-flying aircraft.

The garden and the gallery place Vincent and Françoise in a social and cultural context in which order has been achieved at the expense of vitality, and in which the benefits of this order are conferred on a privileged few. Even the modern communications system is controlled and regulated by the state and serves mainly to alienate people from each other and from their society. Tanner stresses the mechanics of communication: the meter on the pay phone which shows that time is money, the stages in the delivery of a telegram, the intrusion of unwanted junk mail, the reporting of news on radio and in newspapers. Along with images of traffic and pedestrians being regulated by policemen, the concern with mass communications develops a vision of a world in which the creation of order has ceased to be a function of culture (art and religion) and has become purely ideological. The symbol of this world-order is the Swiss cross, which is the emblem of the post office and is displayed on the tail of the Swissair jet that slices its way behind the suburban apartments. It also appears in the large poster that Vincent and Françoise have placed over their bed, coupled with words that relate it to the hierarchy that sustained Charles Dé's father: "Profession, Family, Country."

This poster sums up the values with which the couple are dissatisfied and is perhaps placed over their bed to remind them of the limitations that children would impose on them. Vincent describes their fear of being absorbed into the system through "la petite famille," and it is this fear which motivates their decision to go to Africa. Tanner makes this clear in a group of sequences which summarizes the movement of the entire film. After having identified their fear, Vincent asserts that it is not enough to say that one is afraid. The next shot is a close-up of Pierre Jalée's The Pillage of the Third World, which, we discover, Vincent is reading in the back of a truck on the way to a job. Africa thus emerges as a direct response to the social frustration that prevents him from envisaging his future in Europe (he has had a dream of himself as an old gardener).

But doubts are immediately thrown on Vincent's movement from personal frustration to concern with the Third World by Emilio, a Spanish exile and Vincent's workmate, who is with him in the truck. He points to problems closer to home by asking why the tree they are transplanting should be planted in the garden of a villa rather than in the courtyard of the tenement block in which he lives. The next shot shows the tree being planted in this courtyard while Vincent describes his vision of the tenants resisting the police when they come to chop it down to make way for the new London-Istanbul highway. This small gesture of protest suggests the possibility of practical resistance that is to reappear at the end of the film and foreshadows the failure of Vincent's dreams of the Third World.

Emilio's presence acts as a constant reminder that Vincent and Françoise are in danger of cutting themselves off completely, like Paul and Adeline in Charles. Later, in the back of the truck again, he wonders whether Vincent is prepared to be an alien in Africa as Emilio himself is in Switzerland. He points out that the rich may be at home in exile but that other aliens are people who say nothing and have no political influence. As they work in a garden, Emilio declares that he is not interested in international power politics and that the real struggle is within countries and between classes. When this political harangue is interrupted by the whistling of Marcel, their "non-political" coworker, Vincent remarks that this piece of music does not simply introduce football on television but comes from a work by Purcell. Emilio reproves Vincent for his condescending attitude and reconciles the two men, lightly exposing the intellectual arrogance behind Vincent's radicalism. At this point, Vincent does not understand the lesson but it is reiterated by the friends who come to the couple's farewell party. These friends do not have Emilio's experience, but one of them does tell the couple that they will be taking their problems with them and another warns them that in Africa they will be seen as the rich oppressors.

Since we do not see these friends except in the opening sequence and at the party, we cannot know the basis of their political awareness; but Emilio's insight is clearly based on his own experience as an exile. Vincent does not see that Emilio's description of the exile's political impotence comes close to defining his own frustration. He has become

an exile in his own country but has not been aware of this
because his surroundings have become so familiar to him.
As Emilio and the friends at the party point out, the move
to Africa will make his alienation explicit but will provide
no real basis for overcoming it. Thus, when their contact
in Algeria wires them to wait until they hear from him,
their decision to remain in hiding in their apartment not
only saves them from the "shame" of meeting their friends
but also allows them to live through the experience of going to Africa without leaving Geneva. Moving to Algeria
would mean cutting themselves off from their reality, and
so their isolation in the apartment becomes an image of what
Africa would have meant to them.

The paradox of the title is not simply that Vincent
and Françoise do not go to Africa but also that they do return from there. A similar paradox occurs in the work to
which Tanner's title alludes, Césaire's Return to My Native
Land, in which the poet describes his return to his home
in Martinique after a stay in France. When he wrote the
poem, Césaire was still in Europe and it is his imagined
return that he is able to invest with all the strangeness of
the unfamiliar. In its turn, Césaire's title seems to allude
to Marcus Garvey's "Back to Africa" movement which, in the
early twenties, "argued that the black peoples of America
should go back to Africa and there create with other people
of Africa a continental free state."[4] This movement, like
Césaire's poem, was dedicated to the restoration of dignity
to the black peoples by freeing them from the alien values
of the white man, who, through scorn for their culture and
traditions, turned them into non-beings. Tanner's use of
Africa and the Third World reveals the parallels between the
social forces operating in post-industrial Geneva and the colonial oppression which is exposed by Césaire and Garvey.
The shots of Geneva with which Tanner punctuates the film
stress the modernity of the city and its order, but this society in which all signs of industrial labor (except construction) are hidden is as concerned as any colonial society to
deprive its people of any sense of community or identity.
People are forced to compete for parking spaces, obey policemen and traffic signals, follow the arrows on the road,
and grapple with the logistics of rush-hour travel. The
ability of the forces of order to accommodate almost all contradictions is suggested by a cut from Vincent reading
about the resignation of the commander of the Swiss guard

at the Vatican, to a black policeman directing traffic on a Geneva street.

Isolated in their apartment, Vincent and Françoise undergo the experience of becoming non-persons, an experience which brings into the open the alienation on which international consumer society is based and which its ideology works to conceal. Emilio has already tried to explain this, and it is Vincent's encounter with Emilio after his "return" that drives home the lesson. When he learns that Emilio is to be deported, Vincent calls a friend who is a lawyer, but the lawyer is unable to help because the police say that Emilio has already left. Only after we have heard this do we see Emilio being escorted to a train. The authorities manipulate language and time to create an order based not on physical reality but on bureaucratic convenience. Vincent and Françoise are able to short-circuit this process, however, by using their fictional absence to achieve a detached perspective on the environment that they have previously experienced as "normal" (if frustrating). Geneva is de-familiarized. On their farewell walk by the river, Vincent had already felt that everything looked strange as if they had left a long time ago. This awareness of alienation is intensified by their stay in the apartment when they become completely cut off from the outside world. Françoise stands at a window and sees the people as ants looking for parking spaces. She says that "out there" is Mars, and her feeling of being on another planet is confirmed when she does take a solitary walk in the city. On her return, she tells Vincent that she found the city beautiful but depressing and strange, as if it no longer existed (like Emilio in the eyes of the police).

Even before they have decided to leave, Vincent repeats his routine drive through the city but substitutes Third-World names for the familiar street names that conjure up the "ghosts" of Swiss culture. The superimposition of Algiers or Césaire's Fort de France on Geneva may be another example of Vincent's preoccupation with the Third World rather than the social injustices around him, but the effect is also to reveal the falseness of this dichotomy. The experience of alienation is essentially the same in the Geneva of the developers as in under-developed Africa, and it can only be challenged by working within the society to re-assert the bond between people and environment that has been destroyed. In their apartment, Vincent and Françoise become aware of the impossibility of the complete break with their society implied by their African project. The term of their "exile" depends on the quality of the mail service, and they are equally dependent on the existence of such institutions as restaurants that will deliver food. When the first meal is delivered, they realize that they have forgotten to order cutlery, and Vincent makes a vow not to use a fork until the letter from Africa arrives. Françoise undermines his primitive dreams by ordering the messiest food she can find in a "civilized" menu, and she then persuades him to use a fork out of love for her.

From the beginning, Françoise's attitude to their problems seems to be more balanced and realistic. She does agree to go to Africa with Vincent, and it is she who finds the means to do so by suggesting that they sell their property; but her perspective remains one of almost silent detachment. While she can respond to the beauty of African music, she is not affected by it to the point that she forgets her own culture. Vincent seems surprised when she is easily able to locate a place on the map of Algeria on their wall, and he does not respond to her complaint that all his books on Africa are political. She objects that the books do not deal with the country or the people, and contain no information (for example) on what the women do. When they decide to postpone their departure, he blames the delay on her "Swiss female prudence," but he is clearly trying to make her take the responsibility for his own uncertainty. Her position emerges not as an equivalent to Paul's indulgence of the Swiss national vice in <u>Charles</u> but as a refusal to divorce her words or her dreams from her life.

Vincent's vitality is mercurial: his reluctant agreement to use a fork is immediately followed by an endorsement of modern civilization in his rhapsody on the superb postal service, and this is followed by his frustrated banging on the mail box when the letter fails to arrive. Francoise is a source of stability, but she functions not to pull Vincent back to the center of the social structure but rather to prevent them as a couple from becoming marginal to the point of impotence. She warns him of the danger of dreaming too much, and she extends her demand for full consciousness to their sexual relationship by refusing to make love when he is drunk after the farewell party. Her initial response to his decision not to leave the apartment is to find it ridiculous, and she finally becomes so restless that she has to leave. But, after experiencing the depressing strangeness of the city, she finds satisfaction in being suspended in a vacuum and having time to read and think. If the stay in the apartment teaches Vincent the importance of grounding his aspirations in experience, Françoise becomes more aware of the need for thought and theory to direct experience (as is suggested by her movement from the isolation of the art gallery to solidarity with her fellow-workers at the post office).

The implications of what they have learned in the apartment are developed in an epilogue, nine months later, in which the couple come to terms with their "return from Africa." Far from being "a pointless extension of an already over-long film," as Derek Elley's careless reading would have it, this epilogue applies the film's theoretical concerns to a (literally) concrete reality and relates the couple's social development to the development of their relationship.[5] At first there seems to have been a regression, since Vincent and Françoise are seen in their modern apartment arguing about who should have the car and who will do the laundry. They have become part of the commuting and consuming crowd whose lives are regulated by the needs of the establishment. Yet this dismal reality is at least a more honest expression of the nature of their society than life in their old apartment in the shadow of the cathedral. Their relationship to capitalism had been a naive and inconsistent one, as shown in the sequence in which Vincent sells their car, first pulling a trick worthy of his boss by claiming to be an auto mechanic, and then accepting the first offer from his surprised buyer. Now, their response to the news that they must buy their apartment or face eviction shows a new practical awareness of the workings of the system. They decide to organize the tenants to fight the landlords and, although there is no guarantee that this initiative will succeed, the solidarity with others in the same situation represents an advance on their earlier isolation and desire to escape.

Their decision to have a child also represents an advance on the fears that they had felt earlier, although the film does not rule out the possibility that they may slip into the "petite famille" role that society expects of them. After the tenants' meeting, Françoise seems to be aware of this danger when she suggests that their fighting to stay conflicts with their plan to leave as soon as possible. He says that they will leave as soon as they have won, and then proposes that they have a child to spite "them." In defining "them," he refers to the politicians and merchants of the "cathedral's carillon," those who still pretend that their society is characterized by the sound of bells rather than by the noise of the jets flying over the couple's apartment. He now sees having a child as a subversive gesture, since their child will be "gentle and evil, naive and cunning, and a traitor to its country." The child will thus challenge the concern of society to standardize its citizens and may be able to resolve the contradictions out of which it is conceived. The contradictions are fully expressed in the remarkable moment at the end of this sequence when Françoise, having agreed to have the child, holds her hands over her ears and screams as a jet passes overhead, still smiling nervously as she does so. Out of the sense of triumph at the idea of the subversive child emerges a reminder of the pressures which the child will create for the couple and with which it will itself have to contend.

Despite these pressures, the decision to have the child does raise the possibility of a future in which social and human relations might be less restrictive than they are in the society of the "petite famille" and the large corporation. Early in the film, Vincent describes an Indian wedding in which the couple do not know each other before the ceremony, and speaks of the element of chance involved in marriage. The child will introduce another demand for hard work and another element of the unknown. It will allow them to envisage the future (the child will be fifty in fifty years, says Vincent) but that future must remain unknown (and so Vincent has to face up to the fact that his subversive dreams may not be realized). When one of Françoise's co-workers at the post office announces that she is pregnant, the women speculate about the child's future and discuss the effect on children of pollution and educational brainwashing. Ann, who appears to be the most radical of the women, delivers a "lecture" in which she insists that children are twenty-five years ahead of, not behind, their parents. The severity of her opening words suggests contempt for the pregnant woman, whom she calls an "old cow," but Ann apparently has a child of her own and adds that "kids won't let you lose touch with reality." Like Paul in The Salamander, she sees children as a burden and a restriction of freedom, but also as a means of promoting consciousness-- but only if "old cows" will learn from their children and realize that they belong to the future, not to their parents.

Ann's lecture finishes with her own ironic comment on her "performance" (as does Charles's lecture on cars), and it comes close to the abstract political discourse that Françoise has condemned in Vincent's books on Africa. Yet her words do offer a possible alternative to the "petite famille," based on a breaking down of the elements of possessiveness and conservatism inherent in the bourgeois concept of parent/child relationships. Such a process of contestation implies a new approach to the woman's role, and Ann's aggressive stance is designed to challenge the apparently unquestioning acceptance of motherhood by her co-worker. Françoise, as usual, contributes only a few words to the discussion, but it is in her relationship with Vincent that these issues are most fully developed. While this relationship exists outside the mainstream of bourgeois life, Vincent accepts the idea of male dominance, and it is he who makes the decision to go to Africa. But he often seems to be aware that he is playing a role and it is possible that, as when he blames her for delaying their departure, her relative silence is more effective in directing their actions than his verbosity.

Despite her inwardness, Françoise is less passive than Adeline in Charles and less marginal than Lydie in The Salamander, and she does progress to the point that she can question the basis of her relationship with Vincent. Early in the film, irritated by having to wait for a parking space, he attacks her job because no one ever visits the gallery and she has no time for housework. Her move from the gallery to the post office may be a tacit acceptance of his first point, but it also reflects a growth in awareness that allows her to expose the contradiction between his attitude to her and his concern for the victims of colonial oppression in Africa. In their new apartment, she angrily rejects his complaint that he has no clean shirts and asks him if he takes care of her laundry. While she again acquiesces silently to his decision to have a child (just as she has to his fear of having one), she continues to upset his assumptions by refusing to accept unquestioningly that she will be the one to stay home to look after the baby. Vincent is shocked at the idea that he might give up his job, but she replies that the question may at least be raised. Once the question has been raised, they are able to discuss it rationally and come to the conclusion that there is no rational answer. There is no reason why one should stay home rather than the other, and they finally resort to tossing a coin. The freeze-frame as they peer at the coin to see who has "won" leaves us with an awareness of the limits of reason in dealing with human relationships, but also with a preference for chance over an unexamined acceptance of social conventions.

The social order is seen to be based on an attempt to shut out the irrational, while the purely "political" response to this order (represented by the books on Africa) is equally unable to cope with the complexity of the modern world. Return from Africa reveals this complexity by constantly confronting us with the unexpected and by not allowing us the security of familiar responses. Tanner constructs a humorous fable which de-familiarizes what we usually take for reality and shows an attempt to find a way of life that is rational but also flexible enough to deal with the irrational. The basic tension derives from the couple's attempt to live within society while remaining detached enough to contest its regulation of their lives and to expand the pre-defined space that they have been allotted. The pressures of such a life are not under-estimated, and they appear both in the danger of lapsing back into existing models and in the undignified rhythms of a life governed by the belief that time is money. As they are naked and facing each other, on the night that the child is conceived, Vincent tells Françoise (he remains the master of words) that they will not go to work on the following day. The festive spirit challenges the schedules of everyday life.

The couple's contestation of the social order depends on an ability to distinguish social from natural life. As in Tanner's previous films, nature is associated with the Rhone, which divides Geneva and is spanned by many bridges that suggest humanity striving for harmony with nature. In one image (used three times), a series of bridges recedes into the distance, apparently to infinity; but, in another shot, the actual disharmony is suggested by a construction site encroaching on the river's channel.

This tension between nature and society is epitomized in the first shot of Françoise during her temporary escape from the apartment: a close-up of her face as she walks past a background of trees and parked cars. The cars, the construction site, and the apartment block are the signs of the priorities of social life, while the river and the trees represent the continued, though threatened, presence of nature. The tree planted illicitly in Emilio's courtyard grows miraculously, according to the commentator, in the nine months after Vincent and Françoise have emerged from their self-imposed exile, but it is finally attacked by the establishment. A bureaucrat, an officer in uniform, and a workman are surprised by the resistance of the small tree, which they think at first will be easy to pull down. The tenants do not come out to protect the tree, as Vincent had prophesied, but the thin trunk is still resisting the workman's axe when Tanner cuts to the tail of a jet moving behind apartment buildings.

Realistically and conventionally, we must assume that the tree is felled off-screen, but such an assumption depends on an attitude to the image which Tanner constantly calls into question. On-screen space and time are not seen as a selection from a continuous and coherent reality but as self-contained elements in a structure designed to interact with an audience. The tenuous survival of the tree in terms of what we have seen on-screen becomes a metaphor for the survival, against all odds, of the couple's love and fighting spirit, and Tanner's cutting away from what would conventionally be the climactic moment reminds us of the role of artifice in the structure with which we are engaged. This refusal of the conventional, with its constant baffling of our expectations, prevents the film from settling into a "liberal" ending in which moral uplift derives from the triumph of the human spirit over adversity. Of course, it is possible to wrest the meaning of the film in this direction as, unexpectedly, Bernard Weiner does in his "radical" analysis:

> The ambiguity of the final freeze-frame is merely Tanner's way of saying that the question of who cares for the baby at home is really not that important: this couple is going to make it, without losing their ideals, and the revolutionary potential has thus been strengthened. [6]

But the final image is not ambiguous; it simply deprives us of the resolution towards which the film seemed to be moving. Maybe it does suggest that the result of the coin toss is unimportant, but its main effect is to confirm the film's refusal to allow us to resolve its tensions vicariously through its characters.

From the beginning, Tanner has prevented us from settling into a secure relationship with his images. The title raises the expectation that the frustrations of the couple will be released by their departure for Africa, but this expectation is itself frustrated by their retreat into the enclosed space of the apartment. The restrained treatment of this claustrophobic situation undermines its pornographic possibilities, which are mocked in Vincent's recitation of advertisements for sex films until he is frothing at the mouth. The images are visually so dense that they do not (or should not) become boring, but the duration of many shots and the lack of physical action frustrate any expectations of the kind of easily-consumed film that we see being consumed in the opening sequence. By such devices as the quotations from Césaire, the infrequent and unexpected intrusions of the commentator, the use of minor characters who reappear unexpectedly, the cuts away from the action to shots of Geneva, Vincent's habit of referring to his life as a bad film script, and allusions to other filmmakers (Godard and Pasolini), Tanner makes us conscious of our position as an audience and prevents us from being absorbed.[7]

The point of view of the camera also works towards a consciousness of the nature of the film experience. The slow movement across the faces of the cinema audience is repeated in the credits shot of Geneva and suggests a cool, detached scrutiny. This detachment becomes less cool when intellectual discussions (in the bar after the film, between the boss and his workers, between the four post office employees) are rendered difficult to follow by the rapid pans back and forth with no regard to who is speaking. Our relation to the words and actions of the film becomes as problematic as the characters' relation to their own situations, in which words seem to have become a substitute for action. Vincent feels that they babble on to avoid their problem, but is unable himself to find meaningful words even to begin a letter to Max in Algeria.

The commentator remarks that Vincent and Françoise, as they come to realize that they will not go to Africa, have experienced the withering of words; those spoken by themselves were often too many, those from outside were often lies. They dare not even voice their mutual decision not to go, and language seems to have become completely debased and divorced from action. Vincent's inertia in the morning in the new apartment is expressed when he sits at the table and says he is going but does not move (a point similar to that reached by Charles Dé in his drunken illumination). But words can be renewed by the unfamiliar, as when Vincent's friend (who has memorized Césaire's poem) recites part of it as a telegram to his mother and makes contact with the post office clerk by having her repeat it after him. Language ceases to be the vehicle for official definitions and seeks to challenge and provoke, just as Tanner's cinematic language challenges us by its blend of "realism" and fable, humor and despair, to become implicated in the search for utopia within dystopia.

NOTES

1. Raymond Williams, The Long Revolution (London: Chatto and Windus, 1961), p. 90.

2. John Berger, A Seventh Man (New York: Viking Press, 1975), p. 153.

3. Aimé Césaire, Return to My Native Land, trans. John Berger and Anna Bostock (Harmondsworth: Penguin Books, 1969), p. 39; the translators include Tanner in the list of people they consulted during their work (p. 5).

4. Mazisi Kunene, "Introduction" to the above volume, pp. 19-20.

5. Derek Elley, "Le Retour d'Afrique," Films and Filming, September 1975, p. 41.

6. Bernard Weiner, "The Long Way Home," Jump Cut, 4, November-December 1974, p. 4.

7. The presence of Juliet Berto and Anne Wiazemsky (as

post office workers) and the back-and-forth pans are reminders of Godard, while the long tracking shot in front of the androgynous-looking telegram boy on his bicycle echoes the angelic messenger boy who brings the fateful telegram in Pasolini's <u>Theorem</u> (1968).

6: THE MIDDLE OF THE WORLD

> Landscapes can be deceptive. Sometimes a landscape seems to be less a setting for the life of its inhabitants than a curtain behind which their struggles, achievements and accidents take place.
> --John Berger.[1]

> If a person has been conditioned or has conditioned himself to treat the unknown as something exterior to himself, against which he must continually take measures and be on his guard, that person is likely to refuse passion. It is not a question of fearing the unknown. Everyone fears it, it is a question of where it is located.... To locate the unknown as being out there is incompatible with passion. Passion demands that the unknown be recognized as being within.
> --John Berger.[2]

Tanner's first three films deal with the problems of developing a political language capable of challenging the dominant ideology without resorting to jargon or dogma, and of building an alternative way of life that would not be cut off from the possibility of social engagement. The endings of these films stress the obstacles to the achievement of these tasks but also seem to suggest a movement towards a new and delicately balanced openness: the image of Charles in the ambulance dominates the end of Charles Dead or Alive but he clearly remains unsubdued; Rosemonde's "madness" at the end of The Salamander can be interpreted, as we have seen, as an indication either of her survival or of her disintegration; while the freeze-frame of the coin toss at the end of Return from Africa leaves us with the sense at least of an ongoing struggle.

CHARLES DEAD OR ALIVE

1. Paul (with sledgehammer) confronts Charles and Marianne.
2. Paul (with wounded hand) is confronted by an ambulance man.

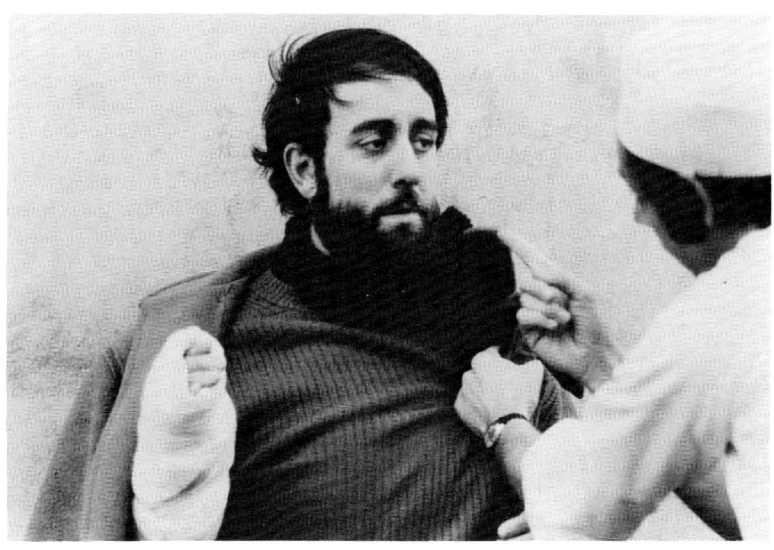

THE SALAMANDER

3. Pierre (left) and Paul play their "game" on a Geneva streetcar.

4. Rosemonde works on the sausage machine.

THE SALAMANDER

5. Pierre and Paul discuss capitalism in the woods.

RETURN FROM AFRICA

6. Vincent and Françoise keep in touch with the outside world.

RETURN FROM AFRICA

7. Françoise and her three colleagues at the post office.

THE MIDDLE OF THE WORLD

8. Adriana sits in the meeting room surrounded by Paul's image.

THE MIDDLE OF THE WORLD

9. Adriana prepares to show Paul "the middle of the world."

10. Paul watches Adriana (off-screen) in the hotel bar.

THE MIDDLE OF THE WORLD

11. Juliette questions Adriana as she waits for the train to Zurich.

JONAH WHO WILL BE 25 IN THE YEAR 2000

12. Jonah scribbles over the mural at the end of the film.

13. Marie describes her situation to Marco's class.

14. Marguerite interviews Mathieu for the job--capital and labor.

15. Max and Madeleine walk beside the Rhone.

16. Marco and Marie check each other out.

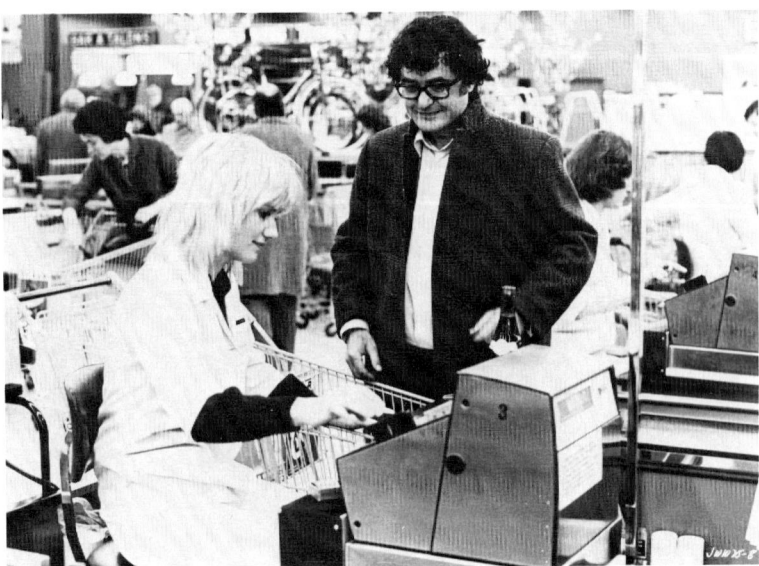

17. Marie (with gun) and Jeanne threaten the old peasant.

18. Jeanne expresses her exultation in the mountains.

MESSIDOR

19. Marie and Jeanne bathe beside the road.

20. Jeanne and Marie in the woods as their journey begins.

LIGHT YEARS AWAY

21. Jonah in the automobile graveyard.

22. Yoshka walks through his domain.

IN THE WHITE CITY

23. Paul's hand reaches out to Elisa.

24. Paul during his wanderings.

Such endings have been attacked for failing to provide constructive answers to the problems raised by the films, but Tanner's strategy with regard to his endings has been effectively defended by Ying Wing Wu in a feminist reading of The Middle of the World:

> His concern with opening his audiences' eyes to the enlightenment--both social and political--necessary for changing our conception of the female experience demands an active evaluation of his characters. Thus Tanner is to be praised for refusing to impose clear, emotionally satisfying endings on his films.[3]

The endings do not resolve (or close) the structures set up by the films but rather confront the audience directly with the tension between despair and hope which provides the basis for these structures. It is not that the endings are ambiguous (as Wu contends) but that the task of interpretation (of selecting a position somewhere between the extremes of hope and despair) is left to the spectator, who must bring his/her own experience to bear within the terms set up by the total structure of the film.

Any interpretation of the ending of the film that responds to its structural system is thus as valid as any other--but also as limiting. The responses of critics to the ending of The Middle of the World illustrate this point and help to suggest the terms within which a structural analysis of the film must operate. The film deals with a brief affair between Paul, a young engineer in a small Swiss town at the foot of the Jura mountains, and Adriana, an Italian waitress in a local café. It is Adriana's final decision to leave Paul and the bourgeois security that he offers her that provides the main interpretative problem. Diane Jacobs asserts that "Tanner agrees that she will undoubtedly end up the matriarch in a large peasant family, no different for this interlude."[4] Whatever the status of the claimed authorial agreement, this interpretation privileges the final image of Adriana in which she is shown eating an orange (as she was when first seen) and speaking in Italian (she has rejoined the Italian community). Ying Wing Wu engages rather with the shot which reveals Adriana working as a machinist in a Zurich factory, now having to deal with a "boss" who talks like Paul but in German, having gained sufficient self-knowledge that "we are now sure that she will not capitulate to the dehumanization of her new job."[5]

Both versions of the ending offer possible resolutions but neither seems to do justice to the tensions set up by the juxtaposition of these two images of Adriana (factory/ home, machine/orange, German/Italian, escape from Paul/ appearance of Paul's double, etc.). Tanner himself offers another version of the ending in which Adriana is seen to be "returning to her class where she will get a better understanding of society." She may be "absorbed and destroyed by production," as Paul has been, but "it is always better to be a worker if you are in industry--you have more capacity for understanding society and for change."[6]

Tanner's interpretation, while not necessarily more valid than any other, does offer a response to both aspects of the presentation of Adriana's situation at the end of the film. It also relates the effect of the ending to the structural tensions set up in the film as a whole, which in turn relate to the tensions found in Tanner's other films. Thus the changing of jobs is a central motif in all his films, reflecting the search of his characters for a space in which they can live. Just as Françoise in <u>Return from Africa</u> moves from being a decorative accessory to the bourgeois consumption of art to a job in which the workings of the capitalist system are more apparent, so Adriana moves from being a sexual object at the café (like Rosemonde in the shoe store) to a position in which the social dimensions of exploitation cannot be evaded. Paul, however, keeps his job despite the political, social and sexual experiences which have exposed its oppressive nature, and he even takes out his frustrations on his fellow employees by intensifying his collaboration with the demands made on them by their bosses.

Paul's attempt to combine his passion for Adriana with the security of his position within the establishment has revealed that society can accept casual affairs that change nothing, but not a passionate and committed relationship. While he outrages his bosses by refusing to conceal his feelings, he is unable to break free of the values that he has accepted by living within the space defined for him by the system. Instead, he tries to draw Adriana into this space (thus attempting to eliminate the "otherness" which attracted him to her in the first place). As Berger explains in a letter to Olympia Carlisi, who plays the role of Adriana, she seeks to enlarge her world by responding to his passion but discovers finally that "he represents what circumscribes her world."[7]

Paul tries to "normalize" Adriana by integrating her into the Swiss bourgeois life-style, a life-style that epitomizes a general attempt to suppress political consciousness. On four occasions the news heard over Paul's car radio describes events which illustrate the apparent diminishing of political differences in the modern world: the Polish foreign minister's visit to the Pope, Castro's approval of détente between the Soviet Union and the United States, the growing friendship between the Soviet Union and France, and the similar friendship between the Soviet Union and Egypt. The illusory nature of this apparent transcendence of ideological differences is demonstrated on a more local level by Paul's election campaign, in which he is presented as a non-political candidate but is manipulated by a party machine concerned only with keeping power. The campaign is planned by a public-relations expert and Paul is given a model speech which he repeats, with calculated variations, at each public meeting. Even the party chairman, who is twice shown introducing Paul at meetings, repeats the same speech, in which he argues that ideologies belong to the past and that modern society needs technicians and organizers rather than politicians. While Paul runs for The Democratic Alliance for Progress and is defeated by the Church Party, the outcome is not related to political issues and the electoral process is shown as one of selling and consumption, of behind-the-scenes patronage and underground rumor-mongering.

The suppression of political discourse is confirmed when Mrs. Schmidt, the café-owner, warns Adriana that a waitress should turn a deaf ear if her customers discuss politics, since business and politics do not mix. One of these customers later complains that the different parties are only out for power. The elimination of real differences from the political arena is related in the film not only to the problems of sexual difference but also to the function of language and communication. Paul's model speech includes a plea for local government to become involved in the protection of the environment, but any attempt to relate politics to the everyday lives of the electorate loses its force in the context of a ritualized language that refuses real engagement with the issues. It is a language that conceals both the cynical attitude towards the election expressed by the party officials in committee and the specialized vocabulary of the expert who gives Paul a text on economic problems, but tells him that the technical terms will have to be removed.

The alienation of the people from the language of power and knowledge is also seen in Adriana's experience: in her working-class environment in Italy she was surrounded by the men's talk of union problems from which she was excluded, just as in the café she must accept being reduced to an object in the crude sex talk of the male customers. The continuity between the sexual and the political debasement of language is captured in the transition from a customer beginning a dirty joke to a conversation between two political organizers who discuss Adriana's sex appeal and finish the joke begun in the café. Paul's passionate involvement with Adriana becomes an affront to the whole social structure because public rhetoric can effect a process of "normalization" only if it is separated from such unpredictable influences as scientific knowledge and sexual passion. Hence the need to create an illusion of unity and consensus while actually compartmentalizing language and experience; hence, too, the demand in Paul's speech that people should moderate their appetites and practice self-discipline.

As Adriana's experience has also shown, the problem of language is complicated by the working of political, social and sexual codes which determine who is allowed to speak. While the women are preparing the café for the (all-male) political meeting, Adriana sits at the empty head-table and begins a speech in Italian. But, of course, nobody hears her, and her only function at the meeting is to serve drinks during the interval. At its height, her relationship with Paul is able to break the language barrier, as suggested by the shot (the only one for February 8) which simply shows them laughing together as they lie in her bed. Shortly afterwards (on March 1) Paul seems to lose his command of words in his public life as he rises to make a speech but stands, uncomfortable and silent, until Tanner cuts away.

The Middle of the World / 111

Paul's loss of control is also indicated by his relationship to the telephone: initially he receives news of his selection as candidate by phone; then it functions as an instrument of his verbal dexterity when he calls to make an excuse for missing a meeting in order to be with Adriana; later, it is used against him when he is woken in the night by an obscene caller; and finally, Adriana's assertion of independence enables her to call him at work to ask him to meet her. The political implications of language are also revealed in the development from the opening, in which Adriana is predominantly silent, through her conversations with Paul in French (his language), to the ending in which she is shown talking in Italian at home while the foreman at the factory (whose words equate him with Paul) speaks German.

The function of language to render experience communicable by organizing it into a system of symbolic signs is seen to have broken down precisely because the arbitrariness of this process has been suppressed. For the purposes of communication, language seeks to give a static form to the dynamic forces of the world, but the aim of "normalization" is to remove the tensions from this process by presenting the static forms as "reality" itself. The result is an illusion of communication which depends on the absence of any possibility of change or difference. It is because he exists comfortably within this ideological framework that Paul can respond passionately to what is different in Adriana, and can even outrage the dubious moral standards of his community, but is unable to conceive any other resolution to his passion than to mold her to fit into his world.

Their affair is an affront to accepted modes of behavior. When he takes her to a luxury hotel, they make love in the bath and sit demurely on the bed dressed only in raincoats as a waiter serves their food. Yet it is also in this sequence that the tensions between them emerge clearly for the first time. He makes plans for her to quit her job so that she can travel with him, while she refuses to make love in the hotel room because it belongs to the rich. Later, he drives her to his house, tells her that his wife has left, and describes the modern conveniences she will find inside; she simply gets back in the car. He is offering to take control of her life, unaware that he is not in control of his own. Just as he tries to possess Adriana, his boss (and party chairman) tells him that "you're my man," and the election defeat binds him even more closely to the social structure as he tries to redeem himself by driving the workers to greater efforts.

The possessive relationships on which society is based are contrasted with assertions of independence that are experienced as madness. After Paul has suddenly appeared at her door one morning to invite her out, Adriana is clearly both puzzled and attracted, and she tells him that he is "mad" (fou). His happiness is expressed by a number of crazy or "irresponsible" acts, but these acts are always held in tension with aspects of the situation which define his euphoria as temporary. As she lies in bed, he dances to the accompaniment of the musical cow that he had given her earlier: the gift itself is a comic hint of his attempt to bring her into the world of possessions, and his essential conventionality is brought out immediately before the dance by his rejection of her suggestion that he urinate in the wash-basin because her room has no toilet. Later the same day he pisses in the middle of a field and then performs a somersault before lying flat out beside a canal, his performance suggesting both the joys of release and the exhaustion that is already beginning to weigh on him.

Similarly, their child-like enjoyment of their escapade in the hotel room is undercut by her sudden awareness of the hotel as part of a political structure. Commenting on Paul's character, Tanner argues that "it is too late for the human in him to cross the line" and that his "playfulness is not enough." It is not enough because he ultimately refuses to take the element of play seriously: "It is up to him to play the game, to go to the end of his passion for her with all that that means, the transformation of his character and life."[8] Because he tries to accommodate his passion to the patterns of the life that he has already established for himself, he grows more and more exhausted from the pressures placed on him, and becomes less and less crazy and irresponsible, increasingly trying to express his desire through material gifts and by molding Adriana into the role of submissive wife. He tries to separate her from her Italian background and from her working-class environment, and is reduced to calling her "mad" (folle) when she asserts her need for her own space by announcing that she is leaving for Zurich.

"Passion is always for the opposite," insists Berger, and the differences between Paul and Adriana (sexual, social, cultural) create a space of desire which initially separates them from a society which works to eliminate passion by eliminating difference.[9] Everything that refuses to be "normalized" is "mad," while "normal" life is seen as one in which desire is channeled into the pursuit of material comforts. Sexual desire is integrated into this system by the central role given to the family in the codification of desire: Paul's wife appears in only one sequence early in the film, but the tone of their relationship is caught in their guardedly casual exchange when she criticizes his tie and he tells her that she can have the car for the day.

Her single appearance suggests the marginal role that his wife now plays in Paul's life (or in the "human" part of his life), even before he meets Adriana, but Tanner does not divert our attention to a psychological study of the causes of the breakdown of the marriage. Their situation suggests that of Vincent and Françoise at the end of Return from Africa, but without the tensions, created by the working-class context, which help to define the earlier marriage. Whereas Return from Africa ends with the anticipation of the subversive child, we only learn that Paul has a child from the public-relations man who supervises the election campaign and who comments that two children would have provided a better image. The dialectical vision of Tanner's films stresses that it is only through tension and contradiction that real relationships can develop, while social structures work to conceal tensions. Charles Dé welcomed the opportunity to work as a way of defining himself against reality, but found that the demands of his job in fact alienated him from reality; Paul's job has provided an escape from his peasant origins, but the security it brings makes his family life into a lifeless structure, not an ongoing process. Boredom in marriage is accepted as a "normal" state of affairs by Paul's political colleagues, but the accepted way of overcoming this problem is to treat sex as just another commodity. His colleagues cannot understand why Paul could not have satisfied his sexual needs with a prostitute, thereby saving his marriage and avoiding scandal.

When they visit his father's farm, Paul tells Adriana that rabbits do not make love in the winter because, for them, sex is not a mental thing. He describes how he used to kill the chickens as a boy, but their distance from the supposedly simple and natural world of his childhood is soon underlined when she jokingly accuses him in a restaurant of trying to buy her with a chicken. Her joke reveals her uncertainty about her sexual identity in a society which offers such extreme alternatives as the "wild times" that Juliette (the other waitress at the café) has enjoyed since the Pill, and the image of the traditional wedding in white that Adriana sees in a store window on her visit to Geneva. Paul's desire for her does not bring him to an awareness of her dilemma, and his attempts to take control of her life only reveal his insensitivity to her needs.

He buys her presents, tells her to quit her job, offers to teach her to fly, to take her to New York, and even to have a plastic surgeon remove the scar on her face. Adriana values this scar, which she received when seriously injured in a fire, as a reminder of her responsibility to herself, and Paul's offer to remove this "blemish" is another example of the way in which the ideology of the consumer society smoothes over the tensions which provoke consciousness. Like the public-relations man, Paul (or part of him) prefers images to reality. Because he has so thoroughly internalized the values of his society, Paul cannot see that he is trying to transform their relationship into a replica of the one he has rejected, and that he is, in effect, colonizing Adriana. Even his efforts to dispense with conventional male roles expose the insidious effects of the dominant ideology: when he cooks her an Italian meal, he tells her that next time he will cook in his own (civilized) way.

Paul's need to assert his social and sexual control is set against Adriana's concern that they should come to "know" each other. As they lie in bed together, she lifts the bedclothes to examine their naked bodies and regrets that not even lovers can know each other completely. Her attitude towards her scar makes it unlikely that this gesture represents (as Diane Jacobs suggests) "a narcissistic appraisal of her perfect body."[10] On the contrary, it indicates her critical questioning of the ways of seeing on which Paul's concern with the perfect image is based. She contrasts her desire to know her lover with the attitude of most men, who think they know a woman if they see her naked and regard their own nakedness as an exposure of their real selves.

As she gradually comes to realize, Paul sees their relationship not in terms of knowledge but of control, and she has to assert her identity and difference. In a later sequence, with the couple in bed again, she responds to his offer to take her to New York by telling him that he does not listen and thus cannot get to know anyone. His only response is to intensify his campaign to gain possession of her, and the next gift is a movie camera. Angrily, she asks him what she should film and cries out that, even if he filmed her inside, he would not know her. She wants him to know who she is and tries to jolt him out of his conditioned responses by playing the role of a whore and by taking the superior position when they make love; but he feels that she is merely being perverse.

The impossibility of "filming the inside" is, of course, one of the basic tenets of Tanner's cinema; but here he examines the danger of responding to this dilemma by accepting the external image as reality. In his election campaign, Paul becomes part of the image generated by the party machine, while the gift of the camera is only one example of his attempt to make an image out of Adriana's complex reality. Her problem in responding to him is that of trying to distinguish image from reality, to discover if his apparent desire for her is different from that of the customers in the café who frankly treat her as a sexual object. When he objects to the way she is treated in the café, she replies that she had had no trouble except from him, suggesting that his inability to relate to her as a subject reveals his own lack of difference from these men to whom he feels socially and sexually superior.

The building up of Paul's public image around the idea of an apolitical objectivity is thus mirrored in the way in which the sexual conventions to which he subscribes function to turn the woman into an object. When Juliette asks Adriana if Paul is serious or if he only wants sex, she cannot answer, and her vulnerability emerges clearly in a sequence in which she shares a meal with Juliette and Mrs. Schmidt. Juliette cheerfully declares that men are happy if women give them what they want, while Mrs. Schmidt warns Adriana not to trust anyone; but Adriana only wants them both not to feel frightened when they make love. As she sits beside Juliette at the station before she leaves for Zurich, Adriana rejects all of her friend's suggestions about her reasons for leaving Paul. There are simply no external reasons in a world in which repression has become so thoroughly internalized.

Mrs. Schmidt's warning against trusting anyone and her concern to separate business from politics show her capacity to operate in a society which lives by appearances (images) but which is actually built on hidden fears and anxieties. Later she is questioned by an investigator about Adriana's honesty and her political activities, but we never learn whether the investigator is working for Paul's party or for his opponents. The murkiness of the supposedly open and democratic political process is from the beginning related to our perception of the relationship between Paul and Adriana. When Paul first sees her during the election meeting in the café, he is seated on the platform and she is serving drinks to the all-male gathering. The camera pans from the platform across the audience as she serves; then we see a medium close-up of Paul apparently watching her, followed by a shot of a green field in spring. Paul's interest in her is distinguished from that of the other men only by the emphasis in the editing, and we cannot be certain that he is in fact looking at her, since the expected shot of the object of his gaze is replaced by the "impossible" shot of green fields (the meeting takes place in January). The connotations aroused by this shot might suggest Paul's inner vision as he watches Adriana, but this romantic possibility is immediately juxtaposed with "reality" as Paul drives his car through the snow and listens to a newscast on the radio.

Our problem here in perceiving the relationship between image and reality is seen as a reflection of "normal" social behavior. As Adriana herself admits, when describing her fears of being badly disfigured after her accident, everyone wants to put on a "show" for other people. In bourgeois society, however, the role of masks in social interaction has become an elaborate ideological sleight-of-hand by which the mask is carefully constructed, presented as reality, and then used as a screen to conceal the actual political processes. While Paul is initially prepared to defy this system by being seen in public with Adriana, the effect of his behavior on his image is brought home to him when he finds a defaced campaign poster on Adriana's door. After his indiscretion has cost him the election, he assures

The Middle of the World / 117

Adriana that he is still "in control," but his actions confirm that he is controlled by his social context. His insecurity is seen in his renewed efforts in his job and in his attempt to accommodate Adriana into the image of himself as a family man that the party machine had been so concerned to project.

The tension between the genuine difficulty of "knowing" another person and the conscious manipulation of images defines the space of social and personal relationships in the film. Paul is associated with the material comforts of his modern suburban home and with the hierarchical spaces of office and factory, Adriana with her small room and with the dingy café where she waits on the men and operates the cash register. Their affair takes place in the countryside (associated with Paul's childhood) and in her room, except for his attempts to impress her by taking her to a luxury hotel and to install her in the house vacated by his wife. He is often shown driving his car and plans long trips with Adriana, but it is she who breaks free by her trip to Geneva and by her permanent removal to Zurich. The sense of an outside world beyond the constrictions of small-town society is suggested by the passing trains which punctuate sequences in the café, reminding us of the train on which Adriana arrived, and anticipating her departure. It is the passing of a train during one of their walks that inspires Paul to lecture her on sound waves and to describe the galaxies speeding away from them. Yet his knowledge of a larger context does not allow him to go beyond the limits set by his everyday life, and he is astonished when she announces her decision to leave (as she watches another train speed into the distance).

A similar set of tensions is to be found in the film's treatment of time. Berger has written that "normal time is longer for an Italian than for a Swiss," and this difference in rhythm characterizes the relationship between Paul and Adriana.[11] Both are controlled by time schedules set by their jobs and both initially experience their passion as a release from everyday time. Paul's friend at the garage expresses shock at his desire to make love in the morning, and the lovers walk slowly through the field or shut themselves up in her room. Although Paul does invent an excuse to miss an election meeting, the pressures of the outside world on the relationship are exerted largely through its demands on their time. Thus Paul quickly has to go back on his promise that they will meet every day, and Adriana has to persuade Juliette to exchange shifts with her. However, Paul's essential acceptance of a social order that defines time as money becomes increasingly apparent, culminating in his attempt to atone for his election failure by improving efficiency and productivity at the factory.

The way in which Paul comes to represent the forces that circumscribe Adriana is underlined by the sequence in which he gives her a watch. She refers to the contradiction between the way he strokes her behind and his objection to the behavior of the other men, and the sound of a train passing foreshadows the end of their affair. The watch (made in the Dé factory?) represents an attitude to time linked to his possessiveness, so that his explanation that the watch records minutes, hours, years, and centuries is logically followed by renewed pressure on her to quit her job. Her experience of time is, however, quite alien to his Swiss precision, being embodied rather in the faces of the old people that she sees on the train when she returns from Geneva, and in the sudden death of Mrs. Schmidt.

This conflict between social and natural time is reflected in the structure of the film. In the opening sequence, the (female) commentator informs us that the film's action will cover 112 days, and each subsequent sequence is introduced by a title giving the date on which its action occurs. But this stress on chronological, linear development is counterpointed by the shots of landscapes at different seasons of the year that punctuate the narrative and place the social pressures on the lovers within the context of the cyclical time of nature. These shots ground the social and sexual relationships within the context of natural rhythms and textures, and Tanner takes advantage of making his first film in color to bring out the sensuous quality of the landscapes and the seasonal changes. The film explores Berger's suggestion that "perhaps the material basis for this correspondence between the natural world and passion is to be found in the nature of sexual energy itself," and the relation of the natural images to the story of Paul and Adriana echoes his comment that "the state of being in love <u>signifies</u> the universe."[12]

Although we do see the lovers in natural settings, the film questions rather than affirms the continuity between their passion and the natural world. The shots of landscapes in which they do not appear function like the non-diegetic inserts in the films of Ozu, providing a contemplative space in which the spectator can consider the feelings aroused by the action; but in Tanner both the space and the feelings are contradictory. We have already seen that a shot of a spring landscape seems to signify the birth of Paul's pasison, but this interpretation is rendered uncertain by the absence of a conventional reverse-shot to establish that Paul is looking at Adriana, and by the initial possibility that the landscape is the beginning of a new sequence (thus signifying a passage of time). Later in the film, a green landscape again accompanies a brief moment of reconciliation in which the triumph of passion seems possible, but (as spring arrives in chronological time) wintry landscapes seem to parallel the breakdown of the relationship. Yet the status of these images remains uncertain, and the effect is to inscribe the implications of the failure of the lovers to achieve the passion described by Berger into the spectator's experience of the film.

The titles giving the date before each sequence (as well as the apparently arbitrary omission of certain dates) and the difficulty of accounting for the order of the seasonal changes work against any sense of natural continuity and make us aware that our experience of time in watching the film is part of a cinematic process. A tension is set up between a detached "structuralist" perspective and the sensuous immediacy of the "realist" treatment of nature and sexual passion. This tension has led to diverse critical assessments, similar to the divergence in interpretations of the ending discussed earlier. For Todd Gitlin the film fails "because the characters have gone abstract and joyless, and so has the style," and because "the direct representation of the body" does not "compensate for the essential anti-eroticism of this starchy, abstract film."[13] Ying Wing Wu, on the other hand, writes of Tanner's "affection and concern for Paul and Adriana" and of "an urgent, tender eroticism not often seen in films."[14]

Such critical differences point to the central conflict in <u>The Middle of the World</u> between human desires and the social structures which try to contain them. Diane Jacobs

suggests that there is a problem in trying to reconcile the
film's "explicitly structural" approach with the depiction of
characters who "work so well as individuals," and Berger
confirms that the filmmakers did set out to make the characters "as specific, as particular as possible":

> The reason why so many love stories fail to convince in the cinema is that the protagonists are stereotypes (or idealisations) and so can never be imagined as provoking the first demand of passion: I want him (or her) because he (or she) is as distinct from everybody else as I am.[15]

In creating this specificity, however, Berger and Tanner refuse to accept Jacobs' implication that it is incompatible with the detached perspective of structuralism. The strategies with regard to time (already discussed), the function of the commentator (not mentioned by Jacobs in her review), and the slow independent camera movements in many sequences, all serve to place the specific relationships in more general contexts. The effect is certainly to create a tension, but this tension provokes an awareness of the tensions in reality between the need for difference that is basic to human desire and the social structures which try to erase all difference.

The function of these structures is defined by the term "normalization," first used by the commentator in the opening sequence to describe the situation in 1974. She calls this "a period of exchange provided that nothing changes," and her assessment is confirmed by the news bulletins heard over Paul's car radio, by the election campaign, and by the outcome of the relationship. The radio announcer describes a political climate of détente between communist and capitalist powers and even claims that the communists are now opposed to spreading the revolution. The "progressives" who support Paul also claim that political differences have disappeared and advocate technological rather than political solutions to social problems. This process of "normalization" also works at the level of personal relationships and is epitomized by Paul's inability to respond to Adriana without trying to "normalize" her in terms of the social context with which he is familiar.

Paul's passion does offer a possibility of change, but he fails to live it out because he comes to accept society's definition of it as "mad." Basically, he refuses to accept that his attraction to Adriana's "difference" requires that he must change. Early in the affair, as she looks at their bodies under the bedclothes, Adriana tells him that they are completely different. He sees only the sexual difference, but she expresses the hope that they will change, not physically but in what they mean to each other. It is now that she questions whether it is possible for them to know each other fully, and her apparent doubts about him are confirmed as he increasingly resists the opportunities for a radical change in himself and thus in his relationships with others. After he has lost the election, he tries to comfort her by insisting that "nothing has changed": he means that the defeat need not affect their relationship, but she realizes that he is locked into the structures of the "normal" world. Although the (female) commentator has described the lovers as having "exchanged hopes," her final comment on Paul is that he knew what he wanted but that his hopes did not allow for any essential change. She adds that perhaps Adriana still "doesn't know what she wants" but at least she "does know what she doesn't want." Her conclusion is that there was no hope for renewal in their fragmented society, so the lovers' hopes were "normalized," just as new hopes are born every day but are shattered against "a wall of opportunism, lies, and fear."

The exchanges between the lovers fail to bring about change or, as the commentator puts it at the beginning, "words, dates, and seasons change but nothing else." This sense of social stasis is reinforced by the fact that the film is set in "the middle of the world" rather than on the margins, with which Tanner is more usually concerned. Geographically, this area is known as the middle of the world because to the south the water drains into the Mediterranean and to the north into the North Sea, and the restaurant in which Paul explains this to Adriana is also called "Le Milieu du Monde." The commentator has, however, already noted that everyone is really the center of his/her own world, and Paul tells Adriana that the region got its name from the fact that he was born there. The joke points to a self-centeredness which is perhaps natural and which is part of the problem of knowing others, but which has become the basis for an ideology that exploits the fear of the different and the unknown, thus neutralizing any possibility of change.

It is this ideology which underlies the process of "normalization," the negation of political differences through a general tendency to move toward the middle of the political spectrum. The ideology exploits fear by equating political difference with war, and the center is thus based on a denial of difference and, consequently, of the possibility of change. Politically, this attitude is supported by the Swiss tradition of neutrality and by the consumer society's conviction that the real problems are technological rather than political. Paul belongs to this center through his job, but his feeling of being in the middle of the world can also be related to his peasant background. Berger has written that, because he "has no choice of locality," a peasant "treats where he is born as the centre of his world" so that "the fact that a stranger does not belong to this centre means that he is bound to remain a stranger."[16] Influences from the past (the declining peasantry) and from the future (the technological revolution) combine to resist the effects in the present of Paul's passion for Adriana. Passion is equated with madness because it threatens to shift the center: as Berger again puts it, passion "constitutes its own centre. And that centre becomes the centre of the world."[17]

After Paul has had the courage to introduce her to one of his friends outside the restaurant, Adriana offers to show him the middle of the world and takes him to her room where they make love for the first time. Their passion creates the possibility of a new perspective on their situation, similar to that which she gained during the period of blindness following her accident. Passion could play the role in Paul's life that "madness" does for Charles, and their "trip" to Africa for Vincent and Françoise. But the pull towards the center is finally too strong for Paul, and he never becomes aware of the way in which his desire is neutralized and normalized.

The dialectical method of Tanner and Berger can be seen in the complex irony that it is Adriana, whose background is proletarian, who, because of her personal and cultural history and because she is a woman, is "still, to a degree, outside the controls of the managerial consumer society," while Paul, who remains close to his roots as a peasant, is firmly entrenched in this society even though, according to Berger, "an intact peasantry was the only class with an in-built resistance to consumerism."[18] Adriana chooses the difficult task of existing on the margins of society but within the circle, whereas Paul is drawn back into the center. As in Return from Africa, several shots of bridges evoke the possibility of a human relationship that might overcome natural and social barriers, but Paul is worn down by the social pressures that prevent him from combining his passion with his position at the center. The final images of Adriana stress the tension between her home life (eating an orange, speaking Italian) and her job (silently working at a sewing machine, German spoken by her male superiors); the final image of Paul shows him driving his car once more up a snow-covered hill.

NOTES

1. John Berger and Jean Mohr, A Fortunate Man (London: Writers and Readers, 1976), p. 13.

2. John Berger, "On 'Middle of the Earth'," Ciné-Tracts, 1, Spring 1977, p. 19.

3. Ying Wing Wu, "The Long Road to Liberation," Jump Cut, 7, May-July 1975, p. 8.

4. Diane Jacobs, "The Middle of the World," Take One, vol. 4, no. 8, p. 29.

5. Wu, p. 8.

6. Lenny Rubenstein, "Alain Tanner: Isolation and Ennui," Film, July 1975, p. 17.

7. Berger, "Middle," p. 25; Berger refers to the protagonists as François and M.

8. Rubenstein, p. 17.

9. Berger, "Middle," p. 17.

10. Jacobs, p. 29.

11. Berger, "Middle," p. 23.

12. Berger, "Middle," pp. 18-19.
13. Todd Gitlin, "Jonah Who Will Be 25 in the Year 2000," Film Quarterly, Spring 1977, pp. 37-8.
14. Wu, pp. 7-8.
15. Jacobs, p. 29; Berger, "Middle," p. 22.
16. John Berger, Pig Earth (London: Writers and Readers, 1979), p. 11.
17. Berger, "Middle," p. 19.
18. Berger, "Middle," p. 23; Berger, Pig Earth, p. 210.

7: JONAH WHO WILL BE 25 IN THE YEAR 2000

> Creativity is one of the most unevenly distributed gifts on earth. Childhood proves this. The first gestures of the child are sheer poetry; he impeccably harmonizes the subjectivity they express with the discovery of a world in which his subjectivity can be objectivized. This harmony is our revolutionary ideal.
> --Report of the commission on "culture and creativity" of the 22 mars movement (April 1968).[1]

> Those who have a unilinear view of time cannot come to terms with the idea of cyclic time: it creates a moral vertigo since all their morality is based on cause and effect. Those who have a cyclic view of time are easily able to accept the convention of historic time, which is simply the trace of the turning wheel.
> --John Berger.[2]

In the final image of Jonah Who Will Be 25 in the Year 2000, the five-year-old Jonah is chalking over the mural created by other children just before his birth. The mural depicts the film's eight major characters who had formed a short-lived commune and had given Jonah his name. Since Jonah represents the possible survival of the spirit of the commune, his scribbling over the mural suggests that he will have to build on, but also go beyond, the example provided by his progenitors. The film's title asserts with apparent confidence that Jonah will be alive in the year 2000, but will he become the subversive child expected at the end of Return from Africa? Or will he be crushed by the pressures of living in a world in which the harmony of subjective desires and objective reality can only be experienced in childhood? The final freeze-frame of Jonah at the wall leaves these questions unanswered and offers a challenge to the spectator, but the complexity and urgency of the issues at stake have been brought home in the course of the film.

Tanner has described Jonah as a "synthesis" of his previous films, and it does weave together many of their concerns into a complex narrative pattern built round the experiences of four couples in a society in which the hopes raised in May 1968 have come to nothing.[3] These couples briefly come together at the organic market garden owned by Marcel and Marguerite, and the birth of Jonah testifies to the possibility of achieving the communal goal of creating conditions in which subjective desires can be objectivized. Childhood is seen as the time during which this harmony is achieved and normally destroyed; and through a network of interconnected images dealing with such issues as time, food, education, and money, the film explores the relationship of nature and society and the struggle to re-define this relationship so that the harmony of childhood can be carried into adult life. The spectator is actively involved in making the connections among these images because the narrative structure is often discontinuous and because this predominantly color film is punctuated by black-and-white inserts which seem to represent the subjective desires and fears of the characters.

The figure of Jean-Jacques Rousseau, that famous "citizen of Geneva," provides one of the contexts in which the relationships among the images can be read. His statue appears in the film's second and penultimate sequences, accompanied by a voice reading extracts from Emile, the work in which Rousseau developed his controversial theory of education as a means of creating the ideal balance between the needs of natural man and those of man in society. The first of these extracts presents an image of human life as a series of physical and moral confinements:

> All our wisdom consists in servile prejudices. All our practices are only subjection, impediment, and constraint. Civil man is born, lives, and dies in slavery. At his birth he is sewed in swaddling clothes; at his death he is nailed in a coffin. So long as he keeps his human shape, he is enchained by our institutions.[4]

Jonah Who Will Be 25 / 127

Although neither Emile nor Jonah advocates a simple return to nature to escape from social constraints, they are both concerned with the way in which "our institutions" organize our experiences of life from birth to old age.

The tensions involved in trying to combine a respect for nature with the need to live in society are made explicit in the film's penultimate sequence, when the camera again circles Rousseau's statue and the voice recites another passage from Emile:

> ... needs change according to the situation of men. There is a great difference between the natural man living in the state of nature and the natural man living in the state of society. Emile is not a savage to be relegated to the desert. He is a savage made to inhabit cities.[5]

Jonah, too, will be "a savage made to inhabit cities" since Mathieu, as his father/teacher, gives up his job at the market garden but keeps his home in the country, despite the discomfort of the daily journey to the factory in the city where he now works. Toward the end of the film, as he rides on his moped through the wintry landscape, we hear his voice singing about the now-dispersed members of the commune and of his determination to keep their hopes together for Jonah's sake.

Rousseau makes a point of including "manual labor" in Emile's curriculum because he wants him to "work like a peasant and think like a philosopher so as not to be as lazy as a savage."[6] Education mediates not only between nature and society but also between body and mind, and the balance of qualities that Rousseau desires in his pupil are precisely those that Serge Daney finds in Mathieu:

> A worker whom a detour through working on the land transforms into an educator, a father whom a detour through a collective deprives of his paternity making him the (future) educator of his son. The transmission is twice de-naturalised by the miraculous assimilation of two enormous contradictions: worker/peasant and manual/intellectual.[7]

128 / A Possible Cinema

In a sense, Mathieu resolves the contradictions that defeated Pierre and Paul in The Salamander and is a more experienced version of Vincent in Return from Africa. He is initially forced to change his job because of the economic situation and his union militancy, but, as often happens in Tanner's films, the change offers the possibility of a new perspective on the social structure. Unlike Adriana at the end of The Middle of the World, he moves away from industry, but the effect is a similar exposure of the social processes which ideology normally conceals. His "return to nature" is only temporary, but it allows him to return to industry --to the factory floor rather than to his previous job as a skilled printer--with a new sense of purpose.

During the communal meal at which Mathilde announces that she is pregnant, it is Mathieu who suggests that the child be named Emile, "for Jean-Jacques." Although his suggestion is not accepted, it is incorporated in what Jonah represents since he inherits something from each member of the commune. In the city, Rousseau is remembered only as a statue which Mathilde passes on the bus on her way to the factory; Jonah restores Rousseau's voice (as one among many) and revives the issues raised by his work. In particular, it uses Rousseau's concern with the relationship of nature and society to re-think the terms within which the political struggle has been developed since 1968. The awareness that ideology passes off social structures as "natural" in origin is linked to another concern of some groups involved in the May events, the ecological problem of what a society that claims to have its origins in nature has made of the natural environment. Mathieu's job at the market garden allows these issues to be raised, but the film also follows Rousseau in stressing the need to break the hold of ideology through the process of education.

In Jonah, the problem of education is defined mainly through the experience of two characters: Marco tries to subvert the public school system from within by disrupting the established ways of thinking and teaching, while Mathieu breaks completely with the system by setting up his own alternative school in a greenhouse at the market garden. Marco's introduction to the film itself disrupts the narrative pattern into which the film seems to have settled comfortably after the disturbing effect of its opening sequences (which will be discussed later). There is an abrupt cut from

Mathieu being interviewed at the market garden to a schoolmaster who introduces Marco (to his class and to us) as the new history teacher. From the back of the classroom, we see Marco place a suitcase on his desk as the students burst into laughter. He takes out a chopping board and a cleaver, noting that his father is a butcher; then, since his mother sings operetta, he takes out a metronome. Finally, he pulls out a length of blood sausage and proceeds to use all these materials as visual aids for his lecture on the meaning of time. His unorthodox approach both defamiliarizes the educational process and makes it more personal (since he draws his materials from his own experience); as the camera moves around the classroom, one boy at the back is reading a book and a girl is knitting, but the rest seem interested.

In three later sequences in Marco's classroom, we are shown more of his attempts to break down the structures governing teacher/student relationships and to relate his teaching to his own and his students' experience. He invites Mathieu to talk about recessions; he allows the students to question Marie instead of giving them an examination; and, when they object to being asked to reveal their secret desires, he tells them that his own secret desire is to sleep with two women. It is immediately following this revelation that he is fired, confirming Mathieu's belief that the system will not allow the truth to be told in schools. Yet, as Mathieu himself comes to realize, it is not just a question of what is told but also of how it is told. When he makes his visit to the class, he sits at the teacher's desk and delivers what Robert Stam calls "a powerfully lucid analysis of the crises and contradictions within capitalism."[8] But, as the camera repeats the movement used during Marco's lecture, it reveals that most of the students are bored and distracted. In contrast, when Marco asks the students to question Marie about her job as a supermarket cashier and the problem of having to live in France while working in Switzerland, a lively session ensues. A student defends his questions about Marie's difficulties with men while hitch-hiking by claiming that he is linking economic history to the history of sexuality. This claim is made playfully and elicits a laugh from the other students, but it does suggest the potential of Marco's approach to make abstract arguments concrete and to encourage students to find relations among different areas of experience.

Shortly after his visit to Marco's classroom, Mathieu sets up his own alternative school for the children who live at the market garden. The sequence which introduces his school is preceded by a series of black-and-white shots in which Mathieu asks the children questions like, "When we move does the moon move with us?" These questions are drawn from those used in the structuralist exploration of the child's conception of the world developed by Jean Piaget at the J. J. Rousseau Institute in Geneva. They suggest that Mathieu now sees education as a two-way process in which the teacher must not lose contact with the student's perspective. He sets up his school in a greenhouse and likens his teaching to "growing flowers," suggesting the need in education for a respect for organic processes like that practiced at the market garden. But just as the produce of the market garden must be sold in the city in competition with chemically-grown produce, so the school is subject to the same social pressures that Marco has encountered. Marguerite is not just the owner of the market garden, she is also Mathieu's employer, and she eventually closes the school because it has caused him to neglect his work.

Marguerite initially objects to Mathieu's plan because it is "not possible" and against the law. However, she tolerates its existence for a year, and the school does not seem to run into trouble with the law. Marguerite finally closes it for economic reasons, since she is unable to pay school taxes as well as Mathieu's wages. Whereas Mathieu feels that the carrots can take care of themselves, Marguerite insists that the children will manage to cope with the school system as they themselves have done. The film does not reject her point of view, just as it does not choose between the strategies of Marco and Mathieu, but it does point to the need for a conscious awareness of the relations between natural and social "reality."

The economic pressures on Marguerite are especially strong precisely because of the extra effort needed to grow vegetables without chemicals. Mathieu's "organic" school is thus sacrificed to the needs of the organic market garden. This underlying economic reality defines what is accepted as possible and explains how we are "enchained by our institutions." In the film's opening sequence, before Rousseau speaks, a man (later identified as Max) enters a tobacconist's store and asks for a packet of cigarettes. He is shocked to find that the price has increased and has a brief discussion of inflation with the salesgirl. At the end of the film, Max will enter the same store and find that the price has increased yet again, thus inscribing the film's narrative time within the time it takes for a packet of cigarettes to increase in price by forty cents. However, when Mathieu explains the high cost of cabbages by reference to "inflation," Marco points out that words like "inflation" and "recession" have been so abused that he has been unable to define them for his class. Mathieu thinks that he knows what they mean and later explains to Marco's class that recession, unemployment, and inflation are elements of a strategy by which the capitalist state keeps workers under control. His presentation is lucid, but the boredom of the students only emphasizes the problem of provoking consciousness of social processes that present themselves as natural and inevitable.

By contrasting inflation with truly natural processes, Jonah identifies it as social and as part of a system which works to limit the horizon of the possible. Max's disillusionment with radical politics after 1968 stems from this closing off of options, as he makes clear in an exchange with Madeleine while they are driving to the market garden. She tells him that he is not wearing a seat belt; he replies that neither is she and that she is smoking; she objects that smoking is not forbidden but he asserts that it will be next year. He suggests that listening to the radio in a car will be forbidden, then talking in a car, and then dreaming; the sequence ends in silence as the car descends into an underpass. Ironically, this bleak vision occurs just before the spirit of the commune is affirmed in the one sequence in which all eight members gather together. The children begin to outline their mural depicting the group, with Max at its center in cruciform position, and (in a black-and-white sequence) the adults imitate the children by rolling down an embankment into the mud. The contrast between Max's vision of the future and this playful episode illustrates the constant collision in the film between actual constraints and what might be possible if they were lifted.

This tension between the actual and the possible is also found in the depiction of Mathilde in the factory and of Marie at her cash-desk. Marie rebels against her situation by undercharging old customers and ends up in prison. The editors of Jump Cut have objected that she acts out of "an individualistic rebelliousness, a politics of sentiment, not of the mind," and they suggest that she should have organized her fellow-workers or the old people instead of cheating the store; but the effect of such arguments is to place radical politics firmly on the side of the existing legal and economic system.[9] Similar criticisms were leveled at the militants of May 1968, and Marie's imprisonment (like the failure of the May movement) does reveal the strength of the forces opposed to social change; but the positive effect of such negative experiences is precisely that they force into the open the constraints that define the possible and make it possible to challenge them.

The constraints placed on Mathilde as a worker are revealed in a shot which shows her working at a machine while a foreman stands behind her with a watch. This image recalls the shots of Rosemonde in the sausage factory in The Salamander, but Mathilde's hands make contact only with metal rather than with the sausage-meat which gives Rosemonde's job its sexual overtones. Mathilde compensates for this lack by her fantasy of working as a masseuse, but she still announces, when she returns home to find Mathieu with his vegetables, that she is "in pieces." When he describes the large apartment that goes with his new job, she immediately wants to have another baby, because she dislikes empty spaces, an empty womb, or empty breasts. Mathilde's desire is later related to the politics of vegetables when she realizes that she is pregnant and asks her son to tell Mathieu that she has "soaked the beans." As with the return to nature, however, the film does not offer Mathilde's maternal instincts as a "solution" to the social issues. The decision to have a child becomes a sign of hope for the future, but it is prompted by Mathilde's alienation from her mechanical job, just as Marcel becomes a hermit in response to the social abuse of nature, and Max becomes a cynic in response to the collapse of his revolutionary aspirations.

Paul and Adriana's relationship in The Middle of the World does not produce a child (and Paul loses contact with his daughter); in The Salamander Rosemonde's illegitimate child is taken from her; and Vincent and Françoise envisage the possibility of creating a subversive child at the end of

Return from Africa. Charles Dé's experience, however, shows that children are not necessarily subversive and that an environment within which subversion is possible has first to be created by challenging the climate of fear which Mathieu describes in his lecture. Jonah, who is biologically the son of Mathieu and Mathilde but socially the child of the commune, represents the continued possibility of subversion. The film's dialectical vision does not replace the industrial process with the natural process of child-bearing but, rather, insists on the need to synthesize both elements of Mathilde's experience.

These elements are also present in the tension set up in Jonah between money and manure. One of the few moments of intellectual agreement between Madeleine, the tantric Buddhist, and Max, the disillusioned radical, occurs when she explains that paper money originated in the retention of feces ("gold and shit, we hide them both") and sees this as the basis of "the Protestant bank." Max is reminded of a friend's thesis that Calvin's doctrine's derived from his constipation, and they both agree that Geneva is "a retentive city." Since Madeleine also attributes Max's reluctance to accept her sexual mysticism to his Protestant upbringing, his disillusionment can be seen as a symptom of the same inhibitions which underlie the system which he opposes. This retentiveness is challenged by the market garden, which refuses to accept modern farming methods that eliminate the need for manure. When the bank sends an agent to make an offer for the market garden as part of a land speculation scheme, he is greeted by Mathieu, who climbs to the top of a pile of manure and announces that he is "the king of shit." Although the agent objects to Marcel's attempt to link the bank's practices to pollution, it becomes clear that a society can be defined by the kind of waste it produces.

Even the respect for natural processes shown by the market gardeners is, of course, subject to social and economic constraints, as becomes clear when Mathieu applies for the job. He first rides his moped through the concrete city of high-rise buildings, urban highways, and traffic noise, and then through the tranquillity of the countryside. But the country is not completely cut off from industrial society since the silence is disturbed by the noise of Mathieu's moped and of Marguerite's tractor. Nor does the natural setting provide an escape from the social relationships of capitalism: Mathieu jokingly tells Marguerite that he is "labor" but that she does not look like "capital," and then finds that as the newest employee he will be given the unpopular task of shifting the manure. The market garden contests the values of a society in which food is sold prepackaged in supermarkets (like the one where Marie works), but its produce still has to compete in the marketplace with vegetables grown more efficiently with the aid of chemicals. Marguerite explains the economic pressures involved in producing food organically, and these pressures mean that the structures of capitalism invade even this oppositional project. When she fires Mathieu, it becomes clear that Marguerite is "capital" despite herself and that she has accepted the implications of running a small business that frightened Paul in Charles (and which presumably contribute to Marcel's reluctance to become involved in running the market garden).

The market garden is situated literally on the margins of the city but is still within its orbit. The produce must be sold there, and the city banker tries to buy the land for a scheme which, he frankly admits, is designed to empty the urban centers and create rural slums. When the banker's agent visits the market garden, he is accused of poisoning the environment with his chemical products. He insists that he is not "in chemicals," but Marcel replies that his "brothers" have destroyed the whales and polluted the water. This exchange exposes the dilemma of the market gardeners who fight pollution but can do so only within the economic structures of the society which creates the pollution. All of the characters face this problem in one way or another: they struggle to create personal spaces that will not be defined for them by the prevailing ideology nor condemn them to the impotence of a purely marginal existence. The market garden becomes a metaphor for the difficult but necessary struggle to engage with, but not be consumed by, the real social processes that govern personal and political experience.

The replacement of manure by chemicals is one of the ways in which society tries to insulate itself from natural processes, but the result is pollution whose effects cannot be escaped. According to Marguerite, there are 27 different additives in a chemically-grown lettuce, and similar amounts are (presumably) to be found in all the food sold in the supermarket where Marie works. Marcel asks the banker's agent if he has ever heard a nightingale sing. The agent replies that he lives in the city and that their children cannot live off nightingales. He also claims that he would eat fish containing mercury and that fish can adapt to changes in their environment. Marcel points out that the human organism is not so adaptable and that the agent's brain would shrivel up, as happened at Minamata. The latter objects to being accused of everything and suggests that they are trying to change the subject. But he finally has to admit defeat when one of the two Zeroes (as Marcel calls his employees) threatens to eat him.

The humor in this sequence sets up a tension between the ideological claim that the different levels of human experience can be dealt with separately and the ecological (and structuralist) argument that everything connects. Marcel describes the discovery of pink islands made up of immense piles of shrimps, which would normally have been eaten by the whales which have been killed to make lipstick. He conjures up a vision of the future in which the human race will die of indigestion through being forced to eat shrimps at every meal. His response to the short-sighted perspective of the consumer society is to become a "hermit"; he sees human beings as the least interesting of animals because they have no mystery. As Marguerite explains to Mathieu, Marcel spends his time photographing animals and then drawing from the photographs, and later we see him shut up in his room drawing from a photograph with a stuffed cat and a chicken on either side of him. Yet he is introduced through a close-up of his hands plucking a chicken, and he continues this task while he expounds on the mystery of animals. This apparent contradiction is intensified by his need to reduce animals to static or stuffed images before he can draw them (just as the city of Geneva has reduced the disturbing memory of Rousseau to the stillness and silence of a statue). In asserting his indifference to people, Marcel does make exceptions for the two Zeroes (because of their "animal" qualities) and for Marguerite (because he sees her as a witch). But he sits back and lets her go about the unmysterious business of running the market garden and pretends not to notice her affair with a "guest worker" from a nearby camp.

Despite the limitations of his position, Marcel's concern with whales becomes central to the film's engagement with the relationship between the natural and the social. During Mathieu's first visit to the market garden, Marcel describes the way in which whales communicate through coded noises which human beings may soon be able to understand, and later Mathieu is shown listening to the sound of whales with the children in his school. It is also Marcel who provides Jonah's name, declaring that he will emerge from the whale that Mathilde has become, to which Marco adds that Jonah will be 25 in the year 2000 when the "whale of history" will disgorge him. As Serge Daney points out, the camera traces the outline of a whale as it moves around the commune members at the table during the baptismal meal, and this sequence is followed, after a caption indicating that "one year has passed," by a shot of whales blowing out water.[10] This shot is in black-and-white, suggesting that whales will soon belong to the past or to the realm of desire and possibility, but it also heralds the arrival of Jonah, who is seen at his mother's breast. The question of the fate of whales is bound up with the nurturing of Jonah, the development of biological and social perspectives that can make possible the survival of the whale and thus of the human species.

The film not only celebrates the existence of whales but also of vegetables. One sequence opens with a black-and-white shot of riot police clashing with demonstrators in the street, followed by a shot (also in black-and-white) of Marguerite declaiming ecstatically in praise of vegetables. The next shot (in color) situates her "realistically," selling vegetables with Marcel to shoppers in an open-air market. The effect is of a dialectical progression bringing the historical reality of social repression into collision with a hymn to nature, and leading to the actual situation in which the poetry of nature and desire is transformed into a sales-pitch. The film tries to make us see vegetables outside the process of economic exchange which has become their everyday context. Thus Marco acknowledges the place of cabbages within the economic structure of inflation, but he also chops one in half to compare its natural structure to the lobes of the brain, and he wants to plant seeds to help his students in the study of time. Vegetable time is also compared with cinematic time when a close-up of Max's hands chopping onions for the communal meal comes shortly after a close-up of a hand planting onions.

Food and eating are key elements in the politics of everyday life. The Zero's threat to eat the banker's agent attacks the present state of "industrial peace" in which, according to Mathieu, workers are eaten alive and turned into "the guts and balls of our enemies." He makes this remark when he decides to apply for the job at the market garden, and as she leaves for work Mathilde asks him not to cook spaghetti for dinner again. She jokingly tells him to "try a vegetable" and when she returns from the factory, she finds him scraping a carrot and sitting at a table covered with vegetables. His exaggerated and enthusiastic response to her suggestion signifies a break with the habitual constraints placed on food and eating by the pressures of everyday life. The pressure has been intensified by Mathieu's discomfort at having to cook for the family, but the new perspective given by his stay in the country is illustrated by his participation, with Marco and Max, in the preparation of food for the communal meal.

Mathieu's transformation is a slightly less extreme version of Madeleine's vision of a break with the routine of office work. She sees (in black-and-white) a male colleague eating food from her naked body, which is sprawled across his desk while work goes on normally around them. This vision is explained later when she tells Max of the role of transgression in tantric rites and mentions the rite of eating impure food from the body of a naked virgin. She also refers to the rite of making group love in a cemetery, but Max objects that she is not a virgin and that cemeteries are cold at this time of year. "Alas," sighs Madeleine, recognizing the conflict of reality and desire.

Max's despondency also disrupts the festive spirit of the communal meal. As the three men prepare the food, Mathieu sings the praises of the "democratic" onion while Marco states his preference for cabbages, but Max is contemptuous that vegetables have become politics. He feels that the situation has only grown worse since 1968 and that the others have accepted the ideological camouflage behind which the signs of social oppression have been concealed. The only alternative that he offers, however, is his declaration that "politics are finished," which he apparently contradicts (even as he says it) by his subversive actions in revealing the banker's schemes to the affected landowners. Similarly, despite his contempt for the politics of vegetables, he does chop the onions for the meal. At the meal itself, he quarrels with Madeleine and is the only one not to join in the song of hope for Jonah. His discomfort and Marie's enforced absence (she is in prison) reveal the disintegration of the commune even as its spirit is affirmed and projected on to Jonah, but Max remains the centerpiece of the children's mural, towering over the others with his arms raised as if he is being crucified.

The film lightly suggests that Max (the dashed hopes of May) "dies" to be reborn in Jonah, but this resurrection will only be successful if the balance of social and natural values can be regained.[11] The need for such a balance also governs the film's treatment of time and space. Tanner's strategy of long takes and self-contained sequences combines a Bazinian respect for "natural" time and space with a Brechtian awareness that our perception of time and space is constructed by social codes. Serge Daney has called Jonah "a reflection on sausage-time and whale-space," and the film's concern is to break down familiar ways of seeing time and space--not to replace them with "natural" ways but to use the natural as a means of de-familiarizing the social.[12] This is also Marco's technique when he uses a string of sausages to illustrate his ideas on time, and (as in the case of onions) the film incorporates the stages of sausage-time, although not in chronological order and excluding the actual making of the sausage (already shown in The Salamander). After Marco has made use of raw sausages, Max and Madeleine are seen eating cooked sausages at a fair, and then Marguerite has a vision of the banker being forcibly removed from his desk and replaced by a live pig.

The time of food, its growing, its preparation, and its consumption, represents the conjunction of natural and social time. One of the main themes of Marco's lecture is that the transition from agricultural to industrial society also led to a separation of social from natural time:

> In agrarian societies people believed that time was cyclical, which accounted for the passage of the seasons. Each winter solstice represented the same moment in time. The individual aged, of course, but mainly because he was wearing himself out. He was the fuel that kept the machinery

of each season working. Capitalism brought with
it the idea of time as a 'highway'--the road to the
sun, the road of progress, etc. The notion of
progress was not simply regarded as one in which
'conquerors' overcame obstacles, winning battles,
but rather one in which the 'oppressors' were specifically chosen for their intrinsically superior
qualities. This superiority could cross the boundaries of cycles and seasons.[13]

Marco exposes the social origins of the unilinear view of
time by using his sausages to elaborate his theory of the
existence of bends and holes in time, while Marcel reveals
the range of natural time in his story of the tick that can
wait for up to eighteen years before it drops on to the back
of a warm-blooded animal but then lives for only one day.

As the film's title, the opening quotation from Rousseau, and Marco's lecture make clear, natural time is manifested in the human experience of aging, but this process
is shaped by our social institutions. After he has been
fired as a teacher, Marco decides to get a job working with
old people because they have been labeled and set aside by
society. Max thinks that Marco will become a vegetable,
but Marco feels that old people know the value of time because all their memories and hopes are in the present. His
attitude grows out of his relationship with Marie, who is
sent to prison for undercharging old people and who has
befriended her neighbor, Charles, a retired engine-driver.
As he listens to Mathieu's talk on recession, Marco sees (in
black-and-white) the classroom filled with old people, while
we hear Mathieu expressing his hope that the students will
be in one piece in the year 2000. By refusing to lose contact with the perspectives of both the young and the old,
Marco reasserts natural time against a social time that divides human life into separate stages centered on institutions (school, family, old people's home), and asks questions that have been suppressed by these institutions.

The concern with aging also figured in <u>Charles</u> and
<u>The Middle of the World</u>, and in <u>Jonah</u> (as in these two
films) social time is based on the premise that time is money.
<u>Jonah</u> is framed by sequences in which time is measured by
the rate of inflation, Mathilde is timed at her job by a foreman with a watch, and Marie tells Marco's class of the pres-

sures placed on her by the time it takes to travel from her home to her job. The effect of such pressures is seen in a sequence in which both Marie and Mathilde are feeling depressed. For Marie, however, the social pressures are intensified by the workings of natural time, since she is having her period, while Mathilde no longer has periods because she is pregnant. Mathilde massages Marie's temples and then covers her up as she sleeps, but in the next sequence Marie is arrested at the supermarket after a frantic attempt to escape down the aisles. The tension between social and natural time culminates in her year in prison, during which, as she tells Charles and Marco after her release, the confinement in space was accompanied by the seemingly slow passage of time.

In order to make us conscious of the rhythms of natural time and the pressures of social time, the film also drawns attention playfully to our experience of cinematic time. Charles compares our experience as spectators to that of passengers looking through the windows of a train, while Marco's vision of old people replacing his students is a flash-forward to his situation at the end of the film. The linear development of the film is disrupted by the black-and-white sequences and by several titles, which seem to reassert the claims of chronology but which make us aware of the process by which our perception of time is being constructed. The opening sequence in the tobacconist's store is followed by a title, "the following morning," which introduces the sequence centering on Rousseau's statue. This title leaves us with the question: what does it mean to say that a statue of Rousseau comes after the purchase of a packet of cigarettes? Everyday time (the tobacconist's), narrative time (the title), and historical time (Rousseau) collide, and we thus experience for ourselves the complex forces at work on and through our perception of time, a concern that will be developed later in Marco's lecture. Similar effects are created by the title, "one year has passed," which links the end of the baptismal meal with the black-and-white shot of whales, and by the final title, "one day in 1980," which again introduces the statue of Rousseau and projects the action beyond the time of the film's making.

This approach to the problems of time and perception encourages us to question the process by which our experience of cinematic time is being structured and to examine actively the relationships between the images. It is this kind of alertness that Marco tries to provoke in his students by his lecture on historical time. He argues, in effect, that historical change is not just a matter of content but also of form, since changes in social structures bring about changes in the cultural perception of time and history. His own view of time stresses the existence of "holes" through which philosophers can see the future and historians the past. He suggests, for example, that Rousseau created "holes" which explain the whole eighteenth century to us. Marco's wit and liveliness turn his history class into a celebration of the diversity of the human perception of time, as opposed to the unilinear view of time on which capitalist society is based and which rejects all other cultural perceptions.

Marco's lecture is, however, divided in two by a sequence in which Max shoots his alarm clock. Previously Max has been seen only in the tobacconist's store and his appearance following Marco's description of the regularity of linear time is as disruptive of narrative time as was Marco's introduction after Mathieu's visit to the market garden. Max is reading a newspaper in bed with a poster of Lenin behind him and piles of books on the floor. He gets up, and the sequence shifts into black-and-white as he takes a gun from a drawer, aims at his reflection in a mirror, but shoots his alarm clock instead. This action may be related to the shooting of clocks in Paris during the July revolution of 1871, which Walter Benjamin sees as evidence of a revolutionary sense of time.[14] Yet Max's behavior seems more suicidal than affirmative, as is confirmed later by his addiction to roulette (which he describes to Madeleine as death, time standing still, the only place where God still exists), and by his prophecy of an oppressive future as his car descends into the underpass. In the context of Marco's lecture, Max's shooting of the clock may be seen as illustrating Octavio Paz's argument that "the idea of revolution ... is undergoing a crisis because its very root, its foundation, the linear conception of time and history, is also undergoing a crisis."[15] Just as Max is unable (according to Madeleine) to break free of his Protestant upbringing, so the idea of revolution which he represents rests on the same linear view of time on which capitalist ideology is based. As they prepare the communal meal, Marco attacks Max for seeing revolution as the sacrifice of the present for the sake of the future and tells him that he will have waited so long that he will be dangerous when the time comes.

Marco's lecture on time ends when he notices that the students are looking at their watches, and he beats out the binary rhythm of the heart on his desk. He tells that that between each stroke there is time and that time is defined by opposition, by the knowledge that the second stroke is not the first. As he urges them to beat faster, he cries out that "in total synthesis time disappears." This idea of oppositions disappearing through synthesis is basic to Madeleine's understanding of tantric Buddhism, and it leads, ironically, to the breakdown of her relationship with Max. At the fair, she tells him that he is still a Protestant because he wants his acts to have effects, and she complains that he complicates things by dividing them in two. Later, on the telephone, she confuses Max by telling him that she wants to cause an explosion in his head, to caress his vagina while he caresses her balls. She wants to break down sexual and moral oppositions and, at the communal meal, she suggests that Mathilde's child be called Siva or Sitka because people are both male and female. She declares that she wants to abolish duality and bring about "a union of the one and the other, existence and emptiness, lotus and mind, vulva and phallus." At this point, Max interrupts her and translates her sexual/mystical fusions into social terms by adding "management and labor, exploiters and exploited" and by claiming that her vision leads to the conclusion that "nothing exists."

Max's bitterness is surprising in view of his own fascination with death and roulette, and, in Madeleine's defense, it should be noted that she does act politically by stealing documents on the land speculation scheme, and that she is last seen in the film helping Marguerite by typing information on chemical additives. Yet Max's point is supported by an earlier sequence in which Mathilde watches a newscaster on television as he speaks of the need for the cooperation of workers and management and then reports on the rejection of labor's demands for participation on the grounds that they are "impractical." The black-and-white television image fills the screen when the announcers addresses Mathilde directly, telling her that there is faith in every atom of existence and that faith is the very essence of things. Television is shown to transmit an ideology based on the apparent abolition of duality, which Mathieu has termed "industrial peace," but the shift to black-and-white creates a tension between whether the personal address represents the underlying message of the newscast or what Mathilde wants to hear. In any case, the affirmation of "faith" is followed by her exultant discovery that she is pregnant, and the sequence thus relates her maternal desires to the workings of ideology.

Another example of the apparent abolition of duality occurs when Charles tells Marco of his activities during the war. He had to drive trains for the Germans and then arranged "accidents," but he is disturbed to find that German and French towns are now adopting each other. The ideological opposition that prevailed in France, but not (officially) in Switzerland during the war, has apparently disappeared in the "industrial peace" of the post-war years. But the film refuses to settle comfortably into the old oppositions which Madeleine calls into question. The strategies of the film can, in fact, be related to Paz's description of the multiple meanings of tantric poetry:

> The basic premise of Tantrism is the abolition of contraries--without suppressing them. This postulate brings on another: the mobility of the meanings, the continuous shifting of the signs and their meanings.[16]

Although Lévi-Strauss has claimed that there is "neither opposition nor contradiction" between Buddhism and Marxism, Paz seems to reinstate the opposition when he claims that "Buddhism offers ... the end of relations, the abolition of dialectics."[17] The film's project is not to abolish dualities or dialectics but rather to expose the oppositions that underlie the false unity that ideology seeks to create. The "mobility of meanings" becomes conscious, and thus undermines the unconscious operations of an ideology which tries to efface contradictions.

In this respect, neither Madeleine's denial of duality nor Max's bitter rejection of her position is adequate, but both are necessary components of the composite and contradictory whole which the commune represents. The unlikely "coincidence" that the names of all the members of this commune should begin with the syllable "Ma" immediately undermines the codes of realism and suggests the need for a more "structuralist" perspective in which the commune is the temporary synthesis of the oppositions among its members. The characters are the children of May or of Marx, but the names also have other connotations which are evoked by the film's concern with natural processes:

> The earth is the body of creation: the word 'matter' comes originally from the same roots as 'mother' (the Aryan ma: to measure, build or construct).[18]

The birth of Jonah confirms the maternal aspect of the commune, while Mathieu's movement from the city to the country provides a framework within which the political hopes associated with Marx and May can find new roots in material reality so that an inhabitable world for Jonah can be constructed. As Todd Gitlin says, "the film intimates the need for a new politics--a politics rooted in love for the material world."[19] Although Gitlin adds that this is a politics "whose actions cannot yet take place," the actual disintegration of the commune does not negate the desirability and possibility of the difficult synthesis which it briefly achieves.

The commune ceases to exist because of the pressures placed on its members by the "real" society in which they have to live and against which they struggle. This "reality" is contested in the film by the nineteen black-and-white inserts, which break the hold of ideology by representing either desires which cannot become actual or actualities which have been suppressed. The latter include the newsreel shots of the army in the streets of Geneva in 1932 which Tanner has resurrected to remind the "Genevan bourgeoisie" of "a little known incident in Swiss history," and the shots of a military May-Day parade in Moscow which follow Max's comment that "politics are finished."[20] These images, like those which embody a desire, are "subjunctive" in that they visualize what is absent from the "official" versions of reality (both capitalist and communist).

Each of the characters is associated with at least one of the black-and-white images of desire (several of which have already been discussed), although they are rarely cued by glances which would root them firmly in the characters' subjectivity. After Mathieu has told Marguerite that she does not look like "capital," there is a cut to a black-and-white shot from behind them as he asks to look at the books to see if the contract is fair. She immediately agrees, and the effect is to suggest the possibility of a new kind of social relationship that would be more in keeping with the subversive implications of the organic market garden. Because Mathieu can only ask his question in a "subjunctive" shot, Marguerite's agreement exposes the fact that in actuality she is "capital," and that her position supports the ideology of "industrial peace" which rejects worker participation as impractical.

The tension between the actual and the subjunctive also comes to the fore in the central sequence in which all the members of the commune come together for the first and only time in the film. It begins with a long take in which the movement of camera and characters creates a choreographed pattern during which the eight friends assemble in the courtyard of the market garden. While the children draw the outline of Max on the wall, Marcel entertains them with a song about how a bear marks out its territory. Marco calls out that "we're all borderline cases," and the euphoric feeling of the sequence does not conceal the fact that Marie's predicament symbolizes the situation of all the characters who are trying to mark out their own personal spaces and to cross the artificial "borders" set up by their society. This long take is followed by a brief black-and-white shot of the completed mural and a close-up (also in black-and-white) of Mathieu apparently looking at it. The retroactive identificaiton of the shot of the mural as the object of Mathieu's gaze suggests that this is the point at which he dedicates himself to preserving the spirit of the commune, but the order of the shots (and the fact that the shot of him looking is also a subjunctive shot) prevents our look from being totally identified with his viewpoint. A similar ambiguity governs the rest of the sequence as, first (in color), the adults watch the children playing on an embankment, and then (in black-and-white), the adults themselves roll down the embankment into the mud. Whether this subjunctive shot is to be related to Mathieu's look or to a more collective viewpoint, it celebrates the playful and childlike elements of the communal spirit and leads immediately into color shots of the market gardeners at work planting onions.

The complex structure of this sequence illustrates the way in which the actual and the subjunctive, constraint and possibility, work and play, continually modify each other and call each other into question. It is this introduction of play and desire into the arena of political debate that accounts for much of the negative criticism that Jonah has received. In particular, Marie's agreement to satisfy Marco's desire to sleep with two women has not been well-received by some feminist critics. There has, however, been little attempt to come to terms with the way this episode is presented: first we see Marco's actual situation as he plays the piano for a group of old people, then a brief black-and-white insert of Marco in bed with Marie and another woman introduces a sequence in which he and Marie prepare to translate the subjunctive into the actual (for this one occasion only). Marie describes the sexual problems inside the prison and then, as they sit naked on the bed, she meditates on the effects of sexual contact on men and women. Since the sequence ends abruptly as the other woman enters, we do not see the actual realization of Marco's desire and are left to consider the sexual issues that have been raised.

This sequence points to the way in which the film tries to place sexual desire and human relationships within a social context. Yet there has been strong criticism that the men in Jonah are defined by their social positions while the women "function rather as 'psychological' archetypes." Tanner has not rejected such criticism outright, but has pointed out that "the respective positions of men and women in Jonah largely correspond to what is still the reality, inside the circle, even on the margin."[21] He has also suggested that "perhaps the major mistake in the film is that Jonah should have been a girl."[22] Whatever the status of the film's sexual politics, however, it is difficult to agree with the Jump Cut editors who write that "the women, except perhaps for the petty capitalist Marguerite ... have no interests beyond their own reproductive organs" and that the film "shows complete ignorance of women's struggles for the last 10 to 15 years."[23] Presumably the violent antipathy felt by these writers to the film prevented them from acknowledging that an earlier contributor to their journal had claimed that The Middle of the World firmly established Tanner as "a leading male commentator of this decade on women's liberation."[24]

In his generally appreciative article on the film, Robert Stam regrets that the women are "not even revealed to be oppressed as women" and feels that "Tanner compounds the problem by having Marguerite rent out her sexual favors to immigrant workers."[25] Stam apparently accepts what the two Zeroes say about Marguerite's behavior, but both times we see her outside the workers' quarters she is with the same man and no money changes hands. The images do not specify the nature of their relationship, but it is possible that the Zeroes are here exhibiting the racist attitudes which Stam attributes to Tanner. He also objects to the brief series of stills showing the inside of the workers' quarters, suggesting that the "photographs of nude women" might confirm racist attitudes and obscure the oppression of the "guest workers." Yet these stills do reveal the sexual dimension of social oppression, as does Marie's account of life in prison, and if Tanner had "ignored the guest workers completely," as Stam would have preferred, he would have run the risk of complicity with bourgeois ideology, which always prefers to repress contradictions. As it is, their living space is seen only in black-and-white and thus is designated as belonging to the repressed areas of experience on which the official version of reality depends.

The inclusion of the subjunctive dimensions of desire and fear subverts this ideologically-defined "reality" as well as the codes of realism that derive from it. As in Tanner's earlier films, the quotations perform a similar function, since they are introduced not to provide authority for the film's arguments or for its reproduction of reality but to multiply the levels of the discourse, thus undermining the expectation of a dominant narrative voice. Even when actual quotations are not being used, the ideas put into play in the text are often drawn from identifiable sources, and, as Serge Daney points out, these ideas have become part of the currency of political debate since 1968. Tanner's achievement lies in giving them what Daney calls a new "strategic effectiveness" by bringing them into new and unexpected relationships with each other and with the forces that resist them.[26] For the Jump Cut editors, all this amounts to, however, is the triumph of Rousseau over Marx and the assurance that "it is all right to drop out and put your hope in your children."[27] Yet the foregoing analysis has amply confirmed Tanner's insistence that his characters are not "drop-outs" but marginals, "connected to the circle if only by their work, while refusing to allow themselves to be sucked into its center."[28]

It is this difficult position which Mathieu tries to sustain in his inner monologue while he rides his moped to the factory. His determination to use the hopes represented by the commune as "levers" to fight social exploitation is balanced by the physical discomfort caused by the cold weather. The sequence ends with a close-up of Mathieu as he wipes away a tear and speaks of the slow progress of change. These final words reinforce Madeleine's complaint to Max that he wants history to move as fast as life. They also refer back to the statement that "you can't stop change," which sounds so promising, coming as it does at the end of the sequence in which the commune comes together, until we realize that the speaker is the banker. Jonah recognizes that radical change will be a slow process and that it cannot be identified with the capitalist idea of "progress." As Matthieu rides into the city, he is stopped by a red light; a close-up of Mathieu waiting is followed by a close-up of the red light which does not change; Mathieu curses the red light, it promptly goes out, and he is able to continue his journey to the factory.

NOTES

1. Quoted by José Pierre, "Create!" in Charles Posner, ed., Reflections on the Revolution in France: 1968 (Harmondsworth: Penguin, 1970), p. 241.

2. John Berger, Pig Earth (London: Readers and Writers, 1979), p. 201.

3. "Entretien avec Alain Tanner," Cahiers du cinéma, 273, January-February 1977, p. 41; in this interview Tanner qualifies the idea of "synthesis" by suggesting that The Middle of the World should be "placed in parentheses," but in another interview he accepts that "on the technical side" of Jonah "there's a lot from Middle of the World, with the use of the camera and the narration done away with"--Lenny Rubenstein, "Keeping Hope for

Radical Change Alive: An Interview with Alain Tanner," Cineaste, vol. 7, no. 4, p. 25.

4. Jean-Jacques Rousseau, Emile, trans. Allan Bloom (New York: Basic Books, 1979), pp. 42-3.

5. Rousseau, p. 205.

6. Rousseau, p. 202.

7. Serge Daney, "Les huit Ma," Cahiers du cinéma, 273, January-February 1977, p. 50n.

8. Robert Stam, "The Subversive Charm of Alain Tanner," Jump Cut, 15, p. 6.

9. Linda Greene, John Hess, and Robin Lakes, "Subversive Charm Indeed!" Jump Cut, 15, p. 9.

10. Daney, p. 49.

11. Christ, of course, compares the period before his resurrection to the time that Jonah spent in the belly of the whale. His words are recorded in the Gospel according to St. Matthew.

12. Daney, p. 48.

13. John Berger, "Jonah Who Will Be 25 in the Year 2000 (an extract)," Ciné-Tracts, 3, p. 10.

14. Walter Benjamin, "Theses on the Philosophy of History," in Illuminations, trans. Harry Zohn (New York: Harcourt Brace and World, 1968), pp. 263-4.

15. Octavio Paz, Conjunctions and Disjunctions, trans. Helen R. Lane (New York: Viking Press, 1974), p. 127; Marco's lecture seems to combine the materialist attitude to history of Benjamin's "Theses" with the philosophy of time developed in a number of Paz's works.

16. Paz, Conjunctions, p. 65.

17. Claude Lévi-Strauss, Triste Tropiques, trans. John

and Doreen Weightman (New York: Atheneum, 1974), p. 412; Octavio Paz, *Alternating Current*, trans. Helen R. Lane (New York: Viking Press, 1973), p. 68.

18. David Maclaglan, *Creation Myths* (London: Thames and Hudson, 1977), p. 41.

19. Todd Gitlin, "*Jonah Who Will Be 25 in the Year 2000*," *Film Quarterly*, Spring 1977, p. 40.

20. Rubenstein, p. 25.

21. See "Entretien," pp. 41-2.

22. Rubenstein, p. 25.

23. Greene, p. 9.

24. Ying Wing Wu, "The Long Road to Liberation," *Jump Cut*, 7, May-July 1975, p. 7.

25. Stam, p. 1.

26. Daney, p. 50.

27. Greene, pp. 8-9.

28. "Entretien," p. 38.

8: MESSIDOR

> It is a film about Switzerland, not Switzerland per se, but more as a kind of symbol of what could happen to the rest of industrial civilisation. We are really further towards succeeding at what everyone else is trying to do with the people ... to integrate them completely into a system and to interiorise this integration into the blood of the people. Apart from small sections who may carry on a marginal kind of discourse, this has really happened now in Switzerland. It's the remarkable 'achievement' of industrial capitalism. There is order, there is peace, there is money. There is consumption, there is everything. So that is the landscape in which the girls move around.
>
> --Tanner[1]

Messidor clearly represents a break with the political and cinematic discourses developed in Tanner's films up to Jonah. The aimless wanderings of two young women through Switzerland are depicted without either the explicit theoretical and ideological analysis or the "subjunctive" dimension that characterized the earlier films. The film seems to be the outcome of a period of personal depression for Tanner that corresponded to the apparent final collapse of the political hopes raised in May 1968. After making Jonah, Tanner said that "this film marks the end of a period of work that I must go beyond," but he also admitted that "I don't know how."[2] The problem of finding a new direction is one that is worked out in Messidor, both in its narrative and in the cinematic strategies through which the narrative is organized.

One of the major signs of change is that Messidor was made without the collaboration of John Berger, who had contributed, directly or indirectly, to all of the previous films. Berger explained that Tanner was "more interested in making films of a looser structure, films which, in a certain sense, were more experimental in their narrative," whereas his own "current thinking about narrative was tighter and more traditional."[3] The actual situation was more complex than Berger suggests, however, since his own stories of French peasant life in Pig Earth (1979) are similar to Messidor in that a theoretical perspective is embedded in narrative structures dependent on characters who lack such a perspective. Berger's distinction between "experimental" and "traditional" forms of narrative tends to break down in a social context which was becoming increasingly conservative and yet still claimed to be truly progressive. The response of both Tanner and Berger has been to abandon the multiple "voices" of their earlier works and to explore new ways of seeing within simpler narrative structures that can expose ideological contradictions.

A "traditional" view of Berger's absence from Messidor was put forward by Gavin Millar, who felt that in the earlier films "ideological didacticism has sometimes been in danger of strangling the director's gift for observed life."[4] Yet the theoretical component in the earlier films does not make them didactic, and the absence of explicit theory in Messidor does not signify that Tanner has reverted to Bazinian realism. Tanner does insist that "the girls have no theory about what they are doing"; but, as Tim Pulleine points out, the film develops an "implicit social commentary" which provides the theory they lack, not in order to explain their actions but to "illuminate our responses."[5] In any case, the limitations of a purely theoretical perspective are already apparent in the earlier films. Jeanne and Marie, the two young women in Messidor, are closely related to Rosemonde, Adriana, and the Marie of Jonah, whose lack of theory increases their vulnerability but also creates a profound challenge to the system by totally refusing its categories. Françoise's criticism of Vincent's theoretical books in Return from Africa, and the disillusionment of intellectuals like Pierre in The Salamander and Max in Jonah also point to the limits of theory, but Tanner makes clear that his rejection of "ideological discourses" in Messidor "does not signify that this is a sphere which I am eliminating from my preoccupations."[6]

The "experimental" side of Messidor is related to some
work that Tanner did for Swiss television during the difficult period after Jonah. Using Super-8 film, he shot
"miles and miles of footage on roads, cafés and landscapes
in Switzerland" and ended up with

> a rather strange and interesting combination of
> absolutely empty pictures which are at the same
> time absolutely crammed with information about
> emptiness, duration, time, the road, the lor-
> ries, etc.[7]

Such "empty pictures" abound in Messidor as Jeanne and
Marie hitch-hike around Switzerland and the camera records
the passing landscape through the windows of the cars in
which they travel. The effect of the television footage
was to renew perceptions of sights which are usually taken
for granted by rendering them unfamiliar, and it is this
unfamiliarity that both fascinates and oppresses the young
women once they have broken their ties with society.

Tanner's "experimental" program provoked no response from its viewers, but he introduces into Messidor
a television program based on an actual series which has
been immensely popular in West Germany and German-
speaking Switzerland. The program invites the public to
help track down criminals, and includes photographs of
the "subjects," interviews with witnesses, and re-enact-
ments of the crimes done "in the pure tradition of the
American TV thriller." In contrast to Tanner's images,
which were "empty" but "crammed with information," the
easy shifts from documentary to fiction in such a program
organize the information according to familiar narrative
codes in a way which Tanner finds typical of television
as an institution:

> Information becomes fiction. Fiction becomes in-
> formation. Every message is mixed up with the
> next one and the result is a kind of brainwash-
> ing and alienation of the people.[8]

In his own earlier television documentaries, Tanner came to
realize that "it was already fiction" and so introduced fictional elements to counter the illusion of an unmediated
reproduction of reality. In Charles, the making of the

television documentary exposes the limitations of the cinéma-vérité approach even though the process does allow Charles to confront the limitations of his own situation; in Messidor, Jeanne and Marie are excluded from the process by which the program is produced. After they pull a gun on a peasant who finds them in his barn, this encounter is re-enacted on television with two actresses dressed like Jeanne and Marie. What we see is a ficitonalized re-enactment of an event which was already part of Tanner's fiction (the substitute actresses are the "doubles" of the film's "stars").

The lack of response to Tanner's "experimental" television program suggests the risks involved in moving outside the circle. Just as Jeanne and Marie are continually pulled back into the circle by their need for food and transport, so Tanner has continued to work within the cinematic institution. While he was working on Messidor, he complained about the effect on cinema of television's demand for "a product that is uniform, standardised and easy," and he referred to the insistence on "the classical kind of narration" as the most insidious aspect of this form of censorship.[9] Tanner seems to comply with this requirement in Messidor, which, as several critics have noted, fits fairly comfortably into the genre of the "road movie." Yet the generic and narrative codes are constantly challenged by the "empty" images, and it is the pressure exerted by the television program that brings about the narrative closure when Jeanne and Marie shoot a man they suspect (wrongly) of betraying them to the police. The problem is not narrative as such, but the kind of actions it is possible to perform and the kind of stories it is possible to tell.

Although the film opens with Jeanne and Marie's declarations of independence and ends with their literal loss of freedom, Tanner uses the conventions of the road movie to open up a space for himself and for the spectator. The freedom normally associated with the open road is here limited not only by the effect of the television program but also by the dependence of the hitch-hikers on other people's cars and by their confinement within the constricted space established by the Swiss border. Unlike the motorists, Jeanne and Marie can leave the roads to explore the surrounding countryside, but their material needs keep pulling them back into the flow of the traffic.

Their experience confirms Charles Dé's verbal attack on cars as part of a system of accumulation which separates people from each other while giving them the illusion that their desires are being satisfied. At the same time, the many "empty" shots of the landscape seen from cars illustrate Charles le Vapeur's remarks on the different perceptions of the driver and passengers in a train. The film defamiliarizes the patterns of traffic and their effect on perception so that we can recognize and evaluate the oppressive structures within which Jeanne and Marie find themselves trapped.

The opening (credits) sequence seems to be a complete denial of the view from the road with which the rest of the film will be concerned. It consists of six aerial shots of the Swiss landscape, smoothly linked through the consistent gliding movement of the camera and accompanied by a Schubert song celebrating the joys of wandering. The lyricism of this sequence culminates in the final shot as the camera soars over snow-capped mountains, but this romantic vision is already being called into question. In the third shot, the camera follows an urban highway which fills the frame with concrete and suggests the alienation from nature of the society with which Jeanne and Marie will have to deal. The sound of a helicopter is heard briefly before the music takes over and acts as a reminder of the technological means by which the romantic effect was achieved, alerting us to the tensions involved in using cinema to expose this alienation and to the strategies that will define our point of view. Although the sequence maps out the terrain which Jeanne and Marie will cover, its allusion to the romantic motif of discovering freedom in nature provides an ironic prologue to a film which, as Karen Jaehne puts it, shows "how the highways and the byways of Switzerland warp an instinct for freedom into a criminal instinct."[10]

The sequence ends with a fade, after which we are brought down to earth with a medium close-up of Marie in a railway station with a moving train filling the screen behind her. The next shot shows Jeanne looking out from a balcony above a quiet street. As she silently bows her head, there is a cut back to Marie, with the train pulling out in the distance. She is searching in her bag, and her first words are, "shit ... my ticket." Marie goes down some stairs to leave the station, and there is a cut back to

Jeanne who now has her back to the street. She tells someone called Alain that she is leaving for the country because she is unable to study in the apartment, and the street behind her suddenly fills with fast-moving cars, their hectic rhythms accentuated by a mirror beside her which creates the illusion that they are driving madly into each other. After Jeanne leaves the frame, we are left to contemplate the traffic for a moment before the sequence ends with a fade. If the opening sequence alluded to the road movie's roots in the romantic "<u>wanderlust</u>," this sequence grounds the narrative in cinematic history with its reference to Lumière's train (leaving not arriving), its Méliès-like illusion (the mirror), and its "primitive" parallel editing. In this context, the off-screen voice of "Alain" acts as a reminder of the filmmaker's hidden presence and of his situation as a man constructing a fiction in which his political perspective will be expressed through the experiences of two women.

The voice of Alain is heard once more during the film, when Jeanne telephones from a café but does not answer when she hears his voice. She jokes to Marie that she was calling the police, suggesting what a return to Alain would mean to her at this point: she then insists that she did not phone at all, revealing an unwillingness to take Marie into her confidence but also testifying to the complete break that she has made with her past life. If Alain's name is an allusion to the director, Tanner's own voice is also heard in the film.[11] It is given to the only driver whose face is not shown; he refuses to give Jeanne and Marie money and delivers a lecture on the virtue of not getting into debt while the two women pull faces in the back seat. As they leave the car, he proposes a sexual "arrangement" by which they could earn the money they need. Since this driver also warns them against leaving Switzerland, Tanner here identifies as typically Swiss a complacency born of affluence which integrates moral and economic values. By lending his voice to the spokesman for Swiss prudence, Tanner once again indicates the tensions in his position as a male of an older generation making use of two young women as catalysts to bring out the violence beneath the peaceful and ordered surface of their society.

The expectation created by the parallel editing that

Jeanne and Marie will meet is immediately satisfied, and the
rest of the film deals with the roughly three weeks that
they spend together on the road. Although the passage
of time is not marked by titles as in The Middle of the
World, each day is clearly defined at the outset by their
sleeping arrangements; later, as the pressures on them
mount, the experience of time becomes much more fluid and
ambiguous. Even at the beginning of their journey, however, there are hints of this breakdown of "normal" time.
On the second day, Jeanne and Marie find themselves beside a lake. The camera tracks away from them and there
is a quick fade, after which the tracking movement re-
sumes until the camera reaches the girls now lying beside
the lake. There is another fade, after which the movement
continues until the camera passes the girls who are getting
ready to leave. During these shots, the quietness of the
countryside is broken only by the distant sound of cow-
bells, and the temporal and spatial disorientation evokes
the girls' feelings of release from the demands of their
everyday lives. Soon the tranquillity of this sequence
will give way to the oppressive sounds of traffic and low-
flying aircraft, and the breakdown of "normal" space and
time will add to the pressures of isolation.

As in the sequence beside the lake and throughout
the journey, the camera remains detached from the action
and there are no point-of-view shots or shot-reverse-shot
figures to encourage identification. Thus when Jeanne and
Marie are getting to know each other, in a café on the
first day and in their hotel beds at the end of the second
day, the camera pans back and forth between them in a
rhythm that seems unrelated to the patterns of their conversation. During their first days together, a number of
extreme-long-shots suggests their feelings of freedom at
having escaped from their limited social contexts into the
vastness of nature. But the distant perspective in these
shots suggests an unidentified observing presence, and
the camera's voyeuristic gaze enforces an awareness that
their escape cannot be permanent. Just before the idyllic
sequence beside the lake, two helicopter shots following the
car in which they are (presumably) riding also combine a
sense of release with disturbing questions about the camera's point of view. Later, we watch Jeanne and Marie
bathing naked in a river, but the next shot reveals that
our point of view is shared by some tourists watching from
the bank.

These reminders of the voyeuristic position of the cinema audience are, however, only part of the "game" played by the camera in <u>Messidor</u>. More frequently, sequences are built up out of a tension between what is shown and what is not shown. When Marie leaves a car to walk across the hills to her village, the camera tracks beside her as she crosses a bridge over the highway; we hear the car door slam and Jeanne calling Marie's name. As Marie pauses for a moment, the camera continues its movement and leaves her behind. The two girls come into frame as Jeanne asks if she can accompany Marie, and they now walk faster than the movement of the camera, which they leave behind. Similar shots are found throughout the film and, as we will see, they culminate in the complex structure of the final sequence.

The camera's "game" depends on the tension between the fixed stare of voyeurism and its own freedom of movement. This tension parallels the paradoxical nature of the "game" played by Jeanne and Marie. Gavin Millar describes how "the freedom of roaming the roads, not having to study, not having to go to work, not having to sit in smoky cafés, becomes the hardship of exclusion."[12] In this respect, the wanderings of Jeanne and Marie confirm the experience of Charles Dé. He initially welcomed his position as head of the family firm because it provided a sense of reality against which he could define himself, but found that his responsibilities isolated him from any meaningful reality. As in the case of Jeanne and Marie, his disappearance is simultaneously an escape from and into reality, and it ends with his being driven back to the city where he will be confined. Tanner's comment on the outcome of Jeanne and Marie's "game" could also be applied to Charles: "... on the one hand they completely disintegrate and, on the other, they find themselves."[13]

After they have run out of money and spent the night in a barn, Jeanne tells Marie that they can either act sensibly and return home or "play a game" by going on without money. They choose the latter course and become outcasts from the affluent society. Later, as they sit beside the road in a city, Jeanne declares that she is fed up with continually passing the same places and that people are beginning to seem unreal to her. Marie assumes that she wants to stop, but Jeanne insists that the journey is just becoming interesting because now they are "crossing the void." When a woman recognizes their faces from television, Jeanne tells her that they are playing "a game of time and empty space" and that the object is to see who will die first. The game is thus in deadly earnest and involves an encounter with the emptiness surrounding a society that believes so firmly in its own moral substance and material security. Jeanne and Marie can only "find themselves" by entering this void and accepting their own disintegration.

The risks involved in this "game" become immediately apparent. Marie insists that they spend the first night in the woods despite Jeanne's fear of wild animals. They spent the next two nights in hotels but, when their money runs out and they become hunted criminals, they are forced to sleep where they can, and the danger comes not from animals but from the men they encounter. On the third day, they are stopped by a policeman who apparently finds it suspicious that they are walking rather than in a car. He asks for their names and gives them a paternalistic lecture on the dangers of hitch-hiking. Jeanne turns the incident into a game by giving false names, but the validity of his warning is driven home in the next sequence. Two men drive them into the woods and attempt to rape Jeanne. Marie's desperate efforts to help her friend are presented in one long take, with the camera remaining at a safe distance. She finally hits one of the men over the head with a heavy stone, possibly killing him. Our detached perspective on these violent acts makes us consider our position in relation to the cinematic spectacle as well as to the social context within which the rape attempt occurs (an extension of the behavior of the men who give rides to Marie in Jonah). As they recover from the attack in a hotel, Jeanne and Marie decide to go on despite what has happened. Jeanne feels that if they stop, it will seem that she has really been raped, and she adds that they are risking nothing because they have nothing.

Jeanne tells the policeman that she and Marie are sisters and that their family name is Messidor. She gives Marie's name as Clio and her own as Thalia. After he has left, she explains to Marie that Messidor was summer in the calendar of the French Revolution and that Clio and Thalia were the muses of history and comedy. Jeanne is a student of history, but her choice of names does not point to any theoretical awareness underlying her actions. The allusion to the French Revolution does, however, act as a reminder of that other revolution which took place only ten years before the making of <u>Messidor</u>; and the attempt to find a new name for summer suggests the revolutionary desire to break with tradition. But summer remains as it always has been and only the history student knows the meaning of Messidor. The revolutionary term has become as archaic as the names drawn from classical mythology with which Jeanne couples it, suggesting that the consumer society has cut itself off not only from nature but also from its historical and cultural roots. Jeanne designates herself as the muse of comedy, not history, apparently out of a recognition that the academic study of history becomes comically irrelevant in a society which denies the meaning of history. It is Marie, the uneducated shop assistant, who becomes the muse of history precisely because she lacks the words to describe her own situation.

In the course of the "game," the psychological aspects of the relationship between Jeanne and Marie are absorbed into a social analysis in which the workings of ideology are presented not in theory but in action. Karen Jaehne suggests that their journey involves the "editing of two personae into a single, schizophrenic personality."[14] From this perspective, the growing solidarity between Jeanne and Marie, culminating in their act of murder, can be related to the "madness" of Rosemonde at the end of <u>The Salamander</u>. She also plays "games" to achieve a freedom that cuts her off from her society, but in the final sequence the commentator places her behavior in the context of the "schizophrenia" of Christmas shoppers.

In <u>Messidor</u>, this social "madness" is related to the divisions within Swiss society. Jeanne and Marie spend much of their time in the German-speaking cantons, and they move through modern cities, quiet villages, and open country. In the background of their desperate journey, tourists move easily through the same landscape, enjoying it as spectacle, consuming it like the images of the television program. Tourism and television are seen as part of an ideological system which works to conceal differences within society and thus creates a kind of cultural schizophrenia hidden beneath a veneer of conformity. Towards the end of their journey, in a village square, Marie remembers that as a child she was amazed that all the people she

saw had their own beds, and she adds that she still feels
the same way. Her own schizophrenic situation is expressed
through the coupling of her fear that she will soon be like
the old woman pushing a baby carriage across the square,
with her realization that she is faint with hunger. The
only alternative to conformity seems to be complete isolation. When Jeanne tells her that she is "completely mad"
for trying to beg from a passer-by, Marie replies that
"they're all mad."

    The woman from whom Marie tries to beg does not
even speak to her, just as an old couple picnicking beside
a busy highway stare blankly at them when they ask for
food. They come to feel that the people they meet are
"unreal," while they are increasingly ignored by other people. Yet some do help, and certain patterns begin to
emerge. The old couple ignore their pleas for food, but
a young German-speaking couple respond readily. An old
peasant threatens to call the police when he finds them in
his barn, but a younger peasant allows them to spend the
night in his barn (and does not call the police as they suspect he will). A man in a new compact car tries to turn
them in to the police, while another in a shabby old convertible offers them a ride only when he learns that the
police are after them. Two motorcyclists pay for their meal
in a restaurant, but some youths in army uniforms recognize
them from television and attack them. In general, the attitude towards Jeanne and Marie depends on the age, sex,
and affluence of the person concerned, and those who help
them are usually marginal figures without a strong stake in
the consumer society.

    The distance between Jeanne and Marie at the begin-
ning is essentially the gap between intellectual and worker
which Mathieu effectively overcomes in <u>Jonah</u>. Whereas
Mathieu is able to extend his political awareness through his
contact with nature, Jeanne and Marie are never able to
translate into social terms the freedom that they experience
in nature. The problems from which each of them is escap-
ing show that personal and social issues cannot be separated.
Jeanne's disillusionment is equally with her relationship with
Alain and with her studies, both of which are associated
with the constricted space of the apartment looking out on
the speeding traffic. Marie is disturbed by the separation
of her parents and can find no satisfaction in her job in a

village store. Despite their different backgrounds, they are both frustrated by a situation in which (as Jaehne puts it) "personal change and social change seem so disparate as to represent a danger to each other."[15]

The impact of their cutting loose from their closed social context stems from the combination of their feelings of alienation with the physical effects of their "game." Jeanne says that hunger makes them aware of all parts of their bodies, and the film stresses the physical consequences of their disintegration. When they drink whiskey beside a mountain lake with the driver of the convertible, Jeanne performs a joyous belly dance, but the sequence ends with Marie vomiting and calling desperately for "help." A similar tension between physical exhilaration and limitation occurs when they climb high up into the Alps. Jeanne looks out across the mountains and stretches her body, declaring that nature creates vertigo and a desire to make love. She touches Marie and asks to be her lover. Marie is disgusted by this proposal and runs off, but she soon follows Jeanne and kisses her on the mouth. There is nothing else in the film to suggest that they develop a sexual relationship, but the sequence ends with them shitting together on the mountain in the setting sun.

The "game" thus brings them close to their natural functions, normally hidden behind social codes and conventions. Their smell becomes so bad that one driver throws them out of his boss's car, and they tell the driver who tries to make an "arrangement" that their names are Madame Pipi and Madame Caca (piss and shit). Given the relationship between feces and money established in Jonah, the heightened awareness of their excretory processes can be related to the way in which their lack of money affects their sexuality. When they first run out of money, Marie suggests that they go to a café to meet some people (as she puts it), but after surveying the middle-aged men in the café, they decide to spend the night in a barn. They refuse the comfortable "arrangement" proposed by the driver who will not give them money for a meal, but they accept a ride from the two motorcyclists who rescue them when they cannot pay for the meal they have eaten. Sex is not mentioned, but the implication that they have sold themselves for the meal exposes the illusion that they can maintain their independence without money. Their situation also exposes what is largely concealed inside the circle: that bodies smell and can be bought and sold.

Their journey involves a confrontation not only with the natural realities that society represses, but also with the violence on which the economic order rests. The gun with which they commit the murder is concealed in the glove compartment of the car of an army officer who gives them a ride on the fourth day of their journey. After he finds that the gun is missing, the officer is unable to pursue Jeanne and Marie because of his respect for the highway code which forbids U-turns on auto routes. Like the gun with which Rosemonde's uncle is shot in The Salamander, the weapon is associated with the hypocrisy of Swiss neutrality and with the militarism underlying the national respect for order. After they have run off with the gun through the concrete pylons of an elevated highway, Jeanne at first throws it away but Marie retrieves it to use as a threat. Since this is the day after the rape attempt, the decision to keep the gun can be seen as a response to sexual aggression, and Jeanne underlines its implications by pretending that the gun is her penis.

They use the gun for the first time immediately after the old couple ignore their pleas for food. In holding up a village store, Marie points the gun at a young woman in a situation similar to that against which she is rebelling. The next morning they threaten the angry peasant with the gun, and it is this episode which is reconstructed on television. The television announcer warns that Jeanne and Marie are armed and dangerous but reassures the audience that they are not suspected of being terrorists. This disclaimer insidiously links the girls to the threat to public order posed by terrorist organizations, and implies that the social tensions exposed in Messidor are those which foster terrorism. The use of the army officer's gun by Jeanne and Marie turns society's weapons against itself, but the threat to shop assistants, peasants and passers-by only serves (with the help of the media) to strengthen the system.

The relationship of social violence to the patterns of traffic is brought out when Jeanne and Marie decide to test the gun. Marie fires into the air as a low-flying aircraft passes overhead and drowns out the sound of the shot.

In the next sequence, a driver tells them of a television news report about a plane crash in Spain; the juxtaposition creates the illusion that Marie may be responsible for the disaster. The driver goes on to relate the crash to the social situation in which there are too many planes and too many cars. His own car is caught up in dense traffic and descends into an underpass (linking the sequence to Max's vision of a controlled future in <u>Jonah</u>). Jeanne feels that, since everybody has to die one way or another, it would be better to do so in a spectacular fashion, but the shocked driver tells her not to joke about such matters. The traffic jam and the plane crash represent the dark undertow of the consumer society, and Jeanne's remark makes clear that the risks of the "game" are an extension of the everyday anxieties that support the social order.

Despite her bravado, Jeanne begins to suffer from nightmares and the "game" takes on increasingly hysterical overtones. After the pair have been seen sitting silently beside a river, there is a fade followed by a close-up of Marie with the river behind her head. The shot is held for some time before Jeanne's hand enters the frame and holds the gun to Marie's head. Marie says that the safety catch is on, but Jeanne denies this and points the gun at her own head. She pulls the trigger and there is a click. The image fades, and then the camera tracks along a wall to reveal Marie sitting in a shelter and Jeanne walking towards her beside the river. Marie is upset because they have spent three days in the same place, with only eggs to eat. They argue, and Marie crushes the eggs she is holding. Jeanne hands her another, which she breaks on Jeanne's head. Jeanne says nothing but simply hands her another, which Marie breaks on her own head, and they both burst into laughter. This incident is almost a parody of the preceding sequence, with the eggs replacing the gun, and the final laughter only signals the end of the "game."

The sequence and the laughter are both cut short by a fade, and then the river fills the screen. This silent shot of the flowing water acts as a reminder of the natural order and is separated only by a brief shot of the girls walking on the road from a shot of an automobile graveyard which represents the social order. Jeanne and Marie emerge from the wrecks among which they have presumably spent the night, and after an argument with a driver who wants to take them to a restaurant attached to a motel, they have breakfast in a roadside café. A male customer seems to be looking at them, and Marie becomes suspicious when he goes into a telephone booth. We see that the man gets no answer to the call, and the situation echoes Jeanne's call to Alain (which she had claimed was a call to the police). We are also shown that the pair have been recognized not by this man but by the chef, who sends a waitress to call the police. The misunderstanding, based on Marie's misinterpretation of the man's look, represents the final breakdown of communications, which is both a consequence of the girls' cutting themselves off from their society and of the ideological structures of that society.

The final movement of the film is introduced by a long shot of the café from the road, with a field on one side and cars and trucks roaring by. This image fades and we see Marie staring off-screen as Jeanne announces the arrival of the police. There is a cut to the café seen from the outside and we hear what sounds like a gun shot before a police car pulls up. The next shot shows two policemen searching Jeanne and Marie inside the café and then we see them being led out to the waiting police cars. This shot ends as a car transporter passes in front of the camera, and only then do we see the body of the man in the café. By not showing the shooting or telling us who pulled the trigger, Tanner stresses not the fact of the murder but its significance in relation to its social context. The murder is pointless but has become almost inevitable. Earlier we saw but did not hear Marie fire the gun into the air, now we hear but do not see the shot that kills the man. The dislocation offers a complete contrast to the omniscient perspective from the helicopter in the opening sequence and, after we have seen Jeanne and Marie being driven away in a police car, the final shot returns to the traffic passing on the road near the café.

NOTES

1. Michael Tarantino, "Alain Tanner: After Jonah," Sight and Sound, Winter 1978/79, p. 40.

2. Lenny Rubenstein, "Keeping Hope for Radical Change

Alive: An Interview with Alain Tanner," Cineaste, vol. 7, no. 4, p. 25.

3. Richard Appignanesi, "The Screenwriter as Collaborator: An Interview with John Berger," Cineaste, vol. 10, no. 3, p. 19.

4. Gavin Millar, "Messidor," The Listener, 28 February 1980, p. 279.

5. Tarantino, p. 41; Tim Pulleine, "Messidor," Sight and Sound, Spring 1980, p. 126.

6. Philippe Defrance, "Entretien avec Alain Tanner," L'Avant-scène du cinéma, 270, June 1981, p. 5.

7. Tarantino, pp. 41-2.

8. Tarantino, pp. 41, 43.

9. Tarantino, p. 43.

10. Karen Jaehne, "Messidor," Film Quarterly, Winter 1979/80, p. 54.

11. See Serge Toubiana, "Messidor," Cahiers du cinéma, 299, April 1979, p. 48.

12. Millar, p. 279.

13. Tarantino, pp. 40-1.

14. Jaehne, pp. 55-6.

15. Jaehne, p. 54.

9: LIGHT YEARS AWAY

> People said for so long that everything was political, that we had to fight religion, or metaphysics or mysticism or whatever. But the thing is that a purely political view of man is a slightly limited one. This doesn't mean that I've become a-political, but just that I recognise other dimensions as well.
>
> --Alain Tanner[1]

Although Messidor involves a break with some of the discursive strategies developed in Tanner's previous films, it is built out of an intensification of the basic metaphor underlying all the films: Switzerland as an image of advanced capitalist society. Light Years Away completely abandons this metaphor, but the result is not a negation of the concerns of the earlier films. Serge Toubiana has pointed out that Ireland was chosen as the location for this film because "it is almost the opposite of Switzerland":

> Ireland is a country of legends, Switzerland a country of signs, completely mapped and banalised.[2]

Ireland thus functions as a metaphor for what is repressed in the highly-developed and rigidly-structured society represented by Switzerland. Whereas Tanner had used the specific signs of the Swiss experience to refer to social developments throughout the western world, now in Light Years Away he was anxious that the specific location should not be recognized in order to create "the idea that all this takes place nowhere, in some garage at the end of the earth!"[3]

The movement from Switzerland to Ireland and from French to English is accompanied by a shift in perspective which allows Tanner to describe the film as "a rejection of ideology."[4] Yet, as we have seen, there has always been a questioning of "the purely political view of man" in Tanner's films, and <u>Light Years Away</u> simply brings to the center one of those "other dimensions" that had previously remained marginal. It deals with one of Tanner's "madmen," an old man who lives in isolation and believes that he will soon be able to fly. This film goes much further than any of the others in challenging our notions of the possible, however, since the old man actually does fly. Although Tanner does seem to have shifted from a political to a mystical perspective, this change is only an extension of the element of "fable" which has always modified the "realism" of his style. In any case, the central concern of the film is not with the miracle of flight but with the relationship that develops between the old man and a young man who becomes his disciple.

This relationship is developed in a context which stresses a continuity with the concerns of the earlier films. The young man is named Jonah. Although Tanner took this name from the novel which was his source, he did include a sequence which makes clear that the action is taking place in the year 2000 and that Jonah is now 25. Yoshka, the old man, resembles Charles Dé, although the ideological basis for his withdrawal from modern society is implied rather than stated. The city in which they meet is Dublin (unnamed in the film), rather than Geneva, but it is introduced through motifs associated with city life in Tanner's other films, especially <u>Return from Africa</u>. A long shot of the city shows heavy traffic crossing a bridge over a river, which acts as a reminder of the natural reality on which the city has been imposed.

These establishing shots of the city occur, however, only after we have seen Yoshka driving through the wild and desolate countryside that surrounds his home in a derelict gas station. Yoshka is associated both with the natural bleakness of the landscape and with the social desolation represented by the gas station, which scars that landscape and which has been abandoned because the country road on which it is situated has been replaced by a modern highway. Yoshka's domain consists of a small shack whose roof is held down by tires, a large shed of corrugated iron in which he keeps his birds, two disused gas pumps, and an automobile graveyard (like the one at the end of Messidor). Its derelict state is an extension of the defaced and dirty apartment building in which Jonah lives and which Yoshka visits to give him the book that excites the young man's curiosity.

Their first brief meeting has taken place in the pub where Jonah works. Yoshka asks him if he is happy with his job washing glasses, and Jonah explains that this dead-end job suits him because he is free to leave whenever he wants. He agrees with Yoshka's suggestion that he is "as free as a bird." After Yoshka's unexpected visit to his apartment, Jonah wanders through a dock-yard and his apparent disturbance is related to Yoshka's influence when he mutters the phrase "as a bird" to himself. His idea of freedom is immediately tested in an argument with his boss, who is annoyed because Jonah did not show up for work on the previous day. He asks if Jonah was sick or if he just did not want to work; Jonah replies that "the idea of washing glasses" had made him sick. The boss promptly fires him, and Jonah's refusal to behave like a model employee relates his situation to that of Rosemonde in The Salamander. Both refuse to accept the social order that governs their everyday lives but, whereas Rosemonde cannot escape from the controlled environment created by Swiss society, Jonah is offered a possible alternative through his encounter with Yoshka and with the mythic landscape.

This alternative involves a rejection of the city. Jonah is inspired to leave by a passage underlined in the book which Yoshka has given him. It describes a character who left the city to discover his own inner strength. Later, when Yoshka sends him on a mission to capture an eagle, Jonah meets another such character. In a speech which Tanner cut during the editing, perhaps because it was too explicit, Thomas, the poacher, explains why he is unable to live in the city:

> I can't stand the streets, the doors, the cars, and all that. I see death everywhere, in the windows of the stores, in the eyes of the people, I see it everywhere. Not a quick, natural death, but rather a slow agony of suffocation.[5]

The productive tension between city and country which Mathieu sought to maintain at the end of Jonah seems to have collapsed completely. The gas station, like the market garden, depends on the city for its economic survival; the building of the new highway has rendered it redundant, although Yoshka still lives there on a small income (presumably from investments) which he later bequeathes to Jonah. Yet, despite his relative freedom from the pressures of economic reality, Yoshka is a contradictory figure, and the movement from city to country does not provide an easy solution to the dilemmas of modern urban civilization.

Although the film's imagery stresses the physical beauty of the natural setting, Tanner also explores the possibilities and limitations of such artificial signs as words. Yoshka's gift of a book to Jonah may be Tanner's acknowledgment that he is for the first time basing his film on a literary source, but the relationship of language to knowledge does become a key issue. Jonah is initially frustrated by (among other things) Yoshka's silence, and one of the first signs of their improved relationship comes when Yoshka asks the young man to read his books on eagles. When Thomas hears that Jonah knows about eagles only from books, he complains that once people simply knew things without having to study them. He objects to the piles of books written about everything and even suspects that one day someone will come to write a book about him. Thomas represents the complete rejection of theory but, since he is already part of Tanner's fiction, his desire not to be studied also suggests (as in <u>Charles</u> and <u>Messidor</u>) that the cinematic apparatus is implicated in the forces of modern life which are being denounced.

Thomas and Yoshka do share a dislike of zoos, and Yoshka also insists on the need for direct contact with nature. He builds his wings according to his observation of the birds that he keeps in his shed, and he cures himself after an accident by lying buried in the ground for three days. When Jonah first arrives at the gas station, Yoshka asks why he should give him what it has taken him his whole life to learn, and the learning-process that Jonah undergoes is based on a series of ordeals rather than on verbal pronouncements. But words do have a place in Yoshka's project: the book is the first step, then Jonah has to read about eagles, and a final phase involves Yoshka questioning Jonah about his experiences on his early-morning walks in the surrounding countryside. Af-

Light Years Away / 171

ter one of these walks, Jonah declares that he now knows why Yoshka knocked on his door and why he came. He cannot put the reasons into words but assures Yoshka that he does know. Words can only approximate to the nuances of human experience, but the attempt to communicate does bring the two men closer together. Just before he takes off, Yoshka tells Jonah that the last few weeks have been the most beautiful of his life. After his death, he returns as a silent presence, but only after once again making contact with Jonah through the words in his will. Jonah is given a series of phrases, and he must read one of them every day, meditate on it, and then swallow it. This ritual resembles Marianne's use of quotations to disturb Paul's complacency in Charles, but here the phrases --"enter into a tree" is the first--have a magical rather than an ideological force.

Although the terms have shifted somewhat, Light Years Away is still concerned with the need to go beyond a constricting social order. When he begins his journey from the city on a bus, Jonah lights a cigarette as he sits beneath a "No Smoking" sign. His rebellion against social regulations begins when he refuses to conform to the schedule set by his boss and loses a job which imposed a mindless routine on him so that the pub could be kept clean and in order. His apartment building shows that this social order is a façade, and it is Yoshka's apparent ability to live outside this order that fascinates Jonah. When he arrives at the gas station, he finds that Yoshka is absent, but he is intrigued by the bird cries coming from the shed and by the disorder of the automobile graveyard. The problem for Jonah, as well as for the spectator, is to decipher these signs in order to decide what Yoshka represents. Jonah is unable to explain what he wants, but he is clearly asking for guidance and a sense of direction. At first, he is frustrated by Yoshka's apparent hostility and his refusal to become his teacher, although Yoshka does take Jonah's money as a "first step" in the educational process.

The possibility that Yoshka is a charlatan or a madman is not dispelled by the series of apparently meaningless tasks which he sets for Jonah. He asks Jonah to attend the pumps in order to show passing motorists that the gas station is open, but a truck driver tells Jonah that the pumps are broken and the tanks are empty. Yoshka then asks Jonah to sort out the scrap metal in the graveyard. Yoshka is annoyed because the scrap is all mixed together, and insists that all that is mixed will be destroyed since things, like people, belong in families. This task hints at the need to create order out of Jonah's own "mixed up" state and suggests that this order may derive from a structuralist perspective on how things relate to each other. The immediate effect on Jonah, however, is apparently negative: he works to the point of exhaustion to divide the pieces of scrap into groups and then has to fulfill the old man's dream that the old metal should be freshly painted. Yoshka is at first delighted with the results but then becomes extremely angry when he notices that a piece of scrap is out of place. He lectures Jonah on the need to do things properly or not at all, and gives him three days to restore the graveyard to its original state.

Jonah is driven to the point of trying to commit suicide, but it is not clear whether Yoshka is testing him or whether he is simply insane. His claim to authority is based on his understanding of nature, but his behavior is distinctly "unnatural" from the perspective of the dominant ideology. When Jonah tries to look after the vegetable garden which is choked with weeds and littered with scrap metal, Yoshka tells him that it is not enough to scratch the surface with the hoe, but that the earth must be turned over in its depths. He adds that Jonah needs violence and love and must lose himself in the earth, himself becoming the manure, the rain, and the sun. This intense identification with natural processes is later illustrated when Yoshka is buried in the earth to cure his wounds and when he becomes like a tree while he meditates. Jonah tries to attain this state and demonstrates his closeness to nature by describing his morning walks to Yoshka. The old man is, however, not satisfied with Jonah's sensitive account of what he sees and experiences; Yoshka insists that he must penetrate the earth and see the shadow which the eye cannot see.

One of the film's strengths (as in <u>The Middle of the World</u> and <u>Messidor</u>) is its insistence on the beauty of what the eye <u>can</u> see. The changing quality of the light is especially emphasized while Jonah carries out his tasks during his stay at the gas station, and the effects of the wind are noted even before they gain a narrative significance through our growing awareness of Yoshka's plans. During their last days together, brief, wordless shot-sequences of Jonah walking in the morning light alternate with his breakfast conversations with Yoshka. Jonah's closeness to nature leads to a closer relationship with the old man, but Yoshka's desire to fly still raises awkward questions about his attitude to nature. In order that he can fly, an eagle has to be trapped, and Yoshka kills his birds and bathes in their blood before he takes off. His scientific observation of the birds gives way to a ritual blood-sacrifice, but nature gains its revenge because the eagle escapes and ends Yoshka's flight by pecking out his eyes. Jonah tells the dancer whom he meets after Yoshka's death that the old man was buried, according to his wishes, without a coffin so that there is nothing between his body and the earth. She is shocked that he would want to be "buried like a dog," but Yoshka has asserted in his will that "each body is the universe."

The problem of evaluating Yoshka's relationship with nature is intensified by his attitude towards women. He tells Jonah that women want to prevent men from flying, and he has broken off his own relationship with a woman because she became too curious about what he was doing in the shed. This woman, Betty, now lives on a nearby farm, and she is the first of three women with whom Jonah becomes involved in the course of the film. When she visits Jonah at the gas station and spends the night in his caravan, Yoshka becomes angry and tells him that he will have to play his "big love scenes" elsewhere. Although Jonah for once defies Yoshka and insists that he will do exactly what he wants, he stays at the gas station and Betty does not appear again in the film. In rejecting women, Yoshka and Jonah are refusing to accept the burden of family relationships which Paul (in <u>The Salamander</u>) sees as a means of self-definition and which <u>is affirmed in Return from Africa</u> and in <u>Jonah</u>. The result is a detachment from reality which the film presents as both a liberation and a limitation.

Jonah encounters the second woman at a dance in a bar during his quest for the eagle. The rock music and stroboscopic lighting contrast with the natural sounds and lighting of the preceding sequences. The frenetic movements of the dancers suggest (as does Rosemonde's compulsive shaking in The Salamander) the way in which popular culture has been invaded by the social pressures to which it is supposed to be an alternative. Jonah dances with a girl and gets into a fight with a drunk who tries to separate them. After the scuffle, there is a cut to the drunk sitting at the bar with his arms round Jonah and the girl. Their reconciliation is not explained, and the sequence ends when the drunk offers to tell Jonah how to find Thomas, the poacher. The potential relationship with the girl is wiped out in a cut from the bar to a shot of Jonah happily climbing into the mountains. Once again, the distractions of sexual desire are rejected in favor of the pursuit of Yoshka's mystical ends. A similar pattern will govern Jonah's affair with the dancer at the end of the film, although Yoshka is now dead and there are suggestions (as we will see) that the influence of the old man is being modified to meet Jonah's needs.

    The relationship between Jonah and Yoshka has developed only gradually in the course of the film. At first, Yoshka seems to keep his disciple at arm's length, and Jonah is denied even the brief glimpses into the shed which excite our curiosity. When Yoshka first finds Jonah sleeping in the caravan, he throws him out, but Jonah buys a pig from Betty's farm as a peace-offering. Yoshka tells him that he has been sold the runt of the litter, and Jonah comes increasingly to feel that he is being treated like the pig. Yoshka asks what good could come from "fattening up" someone as ignorant as Jonah, and he even suggests that the pig is the wiser of the two. In the isolation created by Yoshka's silence, Jonah comes to see the pig as his companion in misery and complains that they are both kept in a state of hunger. When the pig disappears, Jonah finds that Yoshka has cooked it, and the two men come closer over the first meal that they have shared together in the house. They have earlier eaten and drunk together in Yoshka's van during the stormy night that precedes his first abortive flight. Now Yoshka takes advantage of the good feelings created by the meal to recount his dream of the freshly-painted scrap metal. It is his attempt to realize this dream that leads directly to Jonah's suicide attempt, but the growth in the relationship is once more associated with food. Yoshka cuts onions (like Max in Jonah) to treat Jonah's wounds and, just before the successful flight, Jonah is shown sitting sadly at the table which is covered with the remains of their last meal.

The motif of eating as a communal activity recurs throughout Tanner's work and suggests the need to balance social and natural values. The question of whether Yoshka has achieved such a balance remains open. He seems positively demented when he lets out a strange laugh after finding Jonah with Betty, and also on the night of the first storm. Jonah gives a similar cry when he captures the eagle, and it is after his return from this mission that Yoshka shows the first real signs of warmth towards him. By leaving the center of the social circle, Yoshka has chosen to operate on a margin beyond which madness lies. But he tells Jonah that the day will come when he will learn to penetrate things from the center and not from the exterior. Yoshka tries to cross the galaxies and to fly "light years away" from a world which he has already left in spirit; Jonah remains behind to build a new life on the basis of what he has learned while with Yoshka.

This ending has caused some difficulties for critics. Richard Martineau, for example, feels that the sequence in which Yoshka takes off violates the previous stress on the observation of physical reality, and he also complains that Jonah's affair with the nightclub dancer is unnecessary.[6] Yet Tanner has changed the ending of the novel in keeping with his concern to remain "down to earth": in the novel the old man does fly off to the galaxies, while the young man enters a tree.[7] In the film, Yoshka's flight is cut short after about twenty miles, apparently because the eagle pecks out his eyes. The flight is extraordinary, although all but the take-off occurs off-screen, but the natural laws reassert themselves; and the result is a tension between fable and realism not unlike that in Tanner's earlier films. Similarly, Jonah does not melt into a tree, but he does describe Yoshka as resembling "an old tree trunk" when he finds him meditating on his return from capturing the eagle, a state which Jonah himself later attains. As Martineau suggests, Yoshka's flight has not been "prepared for," but the element of surprise involved works not to destroy the film's grounding in the "real" but to call into question conventional ideas of the "possible."

As for Jonah's affair with the dancer, it extends the film's concern with freedom and human relationships. After Jonah has identified Yoshka's body, he is seen wandering aimlessly through the city streets, as he did after Yoshka's visit to his apartment. He crosses a bridge, walking in the opposite direction to the dense crowd (an image that echoes the final shot of The Salamander), and stands motionless amid the noise of the traffic and the garish light of the neon advertisements. The next shot shows Jonah in the dingy nightclub in which the dancer is performing, naked except for a small spangled triangle covering her sex. A short, wordless sequence showing the couple naked in bed is followed by a sequence in which a lawyer explains Yoshka's will to Jonah. The physical relationship of Jonah and the dancer is contrasted with the legal world of books and papers. As Jonah reads the will to the dancer, she comments that Yoshka must have been strange but that she likes his magic. She cannot understand why Yoshka would have asked to be buried without a coffin, but her relationship with Jonah also creates the possibility of "magic" that may extend rather than contradict Yoshka's influence.

The dancer refuses to bury herself "in the desert" by going to live with Jonah at the gas station. He leaves her, as he has left the other two women, and her refusal seems to confirm Yoshka's misogynist attitude. But their parting also undermines the sexual polarity on which the old man had insisted. Jonah asks her if she knows what she is doing in choosing to keep her job and remain in an apartment that resembles the one from which he fled at the beginning of the film. He tells her that she is a "slave," but she replies that she is less of a slave than she would be if she went to live with him. He becomes angry, but then calms down and smiles when she playfully raises her t-shirt to display her sex. This frank sexual gesture reverses the titillating effect of her dancing, in which only her sex remains hidden, and it also recalls a gesture made by Adriana as she tries to persuade Paul to commit himself to his passion in The Middle of the World. Their parting is unlikely to be a final one, and, since she remains in the city while he goes to the country, the tensions created are similar to those created by Mathieu's attempt to mediate between city and country at the end of Jonah.

Jonah still remains under the influence of Yoshka
through the power of words as represented by the will.
If he had simply accepted the physical reality of his relationship with the dancer, he would have been forced to
stay within the confines of the city, in the limited space
allowed to the poor who live near the center of the social
circle; he chooses instead to explore the uncertain reality represented by Yoshka's disembodied spirit. At the
beginning, we saw Yoshka driving his van through the
country to the city; now we see Jonah driving the van
over the same route in the opposite direction. When he
arrives at the gas station, he looks around (as Tanner
puts it in the screenplay), "as if to assure himself of its
reality."[8] After he has picked up some earth and let it
run through his fingers, he begins to clean up the shed
which is littered with dead birds and feathers. As he
does so, he has a brief vision of Yoshka watching him
with a benign smile of approval. This vision again violates the film's stress on physical reality and sets up a
tension with the living body of the dancer as revealed in
the previous sequence. The final sequence establishes
that Jonah now feels at home at the gas station, but the
question of how he will make use of his experience is left
open.

In his screenplay, Tanner introduced another tension
into the ending in a sequence which he decided not to shoot.
After his vision of Yoshka, Jonah was to have had another
encounter with the truck driver who has frequently passed
the gas station. He was to have told Jonah of plans to
build an army base nearby, and to have pointed out that
the army would have to buy the gas station in order to
widen the road.[9] The inclusion of this sequence would
have placed Jonah's "homecoming" in the context of a mili-
taristic society such as that suggested by the use of guns
in The Salamander and Messidor. Its omission points to
Tanner's concern to avoid a specific social context and to
focus on the tensions which have already grown out of the
structure of the film. The existing ending alternates moments of calm with outbursts of intense activity: Jonah
walks quietly through what was Yoshka's room, then he
lets out a cry in the shed, performs a somersault, and
throws earth in all directions; he stands next to the hole
in which Yoshka was buried and then suddenly yells that
he has seen him; the camera pans slowly around the gas

station and comes to rest on the eagle perched on one of
the pumps; and finally, Jonah is shown smiling happily.
 As in all of the earlier films, the ending is open.
The separation of Jonah and the dancer recalls the separation of Paul and Adriana at the end of The Middle of the
World, while the suggestion of madness echoes the endings
of Charles, The Salamander, and Messidor. In his interview with Tanner, Philippe Defrance links "the death of
Yoshka to the failure of the characters in Jonah, to the
rupture in The Middle of the World, to the end of Messidor,
to the incarceration of Charles in Charles Dead or Alive."
He suggests that Tanner's vision is one in which "marginality, utopia or desire are always crushed, normalised,
killed."[10] Tanner insists that his films are not pessimistic
and that the apparent failures always lead to a gain in
consciousness. The situation in the year 2000 at the end
of Light Years Away may be bleaker than in any previous
Tanner film, but the tension between the real and the
possible still remains as a challenge to which the spectator
must respond.

NOTES

1. Jill Forbes, "Interview with Alain Tanner," Films and Filming, February 1982, p. 20.

2. Serge Toubiana, quoted in the edition of the screen-play published (as Les Années lumière) in L'Avant-scène du cinéma, 270, June 1981, p. 55.

3. Forbes, p. 21.

4. Forbes, p. 20.

5. L'Avant-scène, p. 44.

6. Richard Martineau, "Les Années lumière," Séquences, 107, January 1982, p. 38.

7. Philippe Defrance, "Entretien avec Alain Tanner," L'Avant-scène du cinéma, 270, June 1981, p. 6.

8. L'Avant-scène, p. 50.

9. The sequence is printed in L'Avant-scène, p. 50.

10. Defrance, p. 6.

10: CONCLUSION: TANNER WHO WILL BE 70 IN THE YEAR 2000

> There is ... a deep current which makes it likely that this birth of Swiss cinema will not resemble the multiple births that took place in 1910, 1920, 1925, 1930, etc. This cinema is now created by young people who are not trying to compete with the methods of Hollywood or of the film industry, but who have realised that the attempt to establish a Swiss cinema requires the treatment of the problems of Switzerland today, with the means that are available to us....
> --Freddy Buache, 1969[1]

> Messidor was my last film on the subject of Switzerland.
> --Alain Tanner, 1983[2]

Tanner's most recent film, In the White City (1983), is his second film made outside Switzerland. It is a Swiss-Portuguese co-production and deals with the experiences of a German-Swiss seaman in Lisbon. Since Tanner was himself a merchant seaman before he became a filmmaker, the film can be seen as a return to his origins and has been called his "second first film."[3] Yet there are many points of contact with the earlier films: the depiction of Lisbon through the eyes of an exile points back to the defamiliarization of Geneva in Return from Africa, while the seaman's affair with a Portuguese woman extends the concern with the relationship between cultural and sexual codes developed in The Middle of the World.

The link between Tanner and Paul, the seaman, is reinforced by the Super-8 camera with which Paul records his visit. Grainy "home-movie" shots from this camera are contrasted throughout with the film's basic 35mm. images.

Conclusion / 181

The camera within the film reminds us of the film's own production process, as it does in the openings of Charles and The Middle of the World; but the image-making process is now no longer controlled by institutions as it is in Charles and Messidor, nor is the possession of a camera a sign of status and power as it is for Paul in The Middle of the World.

The final image of In the White City shows a young woman sitting opposite Paul in a train compartment as he travels home. This image begins in 35mm. but shifts into Super-8, even though Paul has previously lost his camera. Tanner has described this shot as suggesting that "romantic perception has become totally subjective," but it also projects a fantasy of being able to create images without material support.[4] Paul is returning to the hostile reality of Switzerland, and this final image can be read as a challenge to conventional notions of the possible (like the fantastic elements in Light Years Away). Tanner, however, is very much aware that unmediated perception is a fantasy and that he still has to find backing in order to make his films possible. His own alienation from what Switzerland represents has become so intense that he feels "condemned to wander, like Paul ... in search of new visions."[5]

The presence of the Super-8 camera in In the White City (and its absence in the final shot) relates to an ongoing tension in Tanner's cinema. After making Charles (in 16mm.), he rejected the arguments of those young critics who felt that the new Swiss cinema had already been "assimilated by the system" and who preferred to make 8mm. "underground" films.[6] Yet he himself used Super-8 to shoot the "absolutely empty pictures" of the television program that he worked on after making Jonah.[7] As we have seen, the lack of response to this program seems to have convinced Tanner of the futility of such marginal practices within an institution typified by the kind of popular program seen in Messidor. His own filmmaking strategies have normally accepted the commercial 35mm. format but have also been built around the insistence that "the camera is a heavy, clumsy instrument, quite the opposite of the eye."[8] Tanner's refusal to make the camera "invisible" through the use of the classical codes of editing makes explicit his awareness of the material burdens of a filmmaking practice that wishes to remain within the circle.

The transformation of Paul's visible camera into an invisible one thus becomes an ironic allusion to the equation of camera and eye on which the classical codes are based.

In the earlier films, the burden of the camera, accepted to avoid a marginal discourse, is accompanied by the burden of living in Switzerland. The new Swiss cinema had set out to make films that would be culturally and economically appropriate to the Swiss context, and Tanner uses the Swiss experience of living "on the frontier" as the basis for a political vision that grows out of the events of May 1968. This vision is most fully expressed in Jonah, but the insidious pressures of Swiss conservatism are seen at their most severe in Messidor. The imprisonment of the two women inside the Swiss borders can be seen as a reflection of Tanner's own frustrations. Yet he has himself said that Switzerland in this film is "a kind of symbol of what could happen to the rest of industrial civilisation."[9] The "fear of change," which Tanner attributed to the Swiss in 1970, has come to dominate the social and cultural climate of the late seventies and the eighties; and Tanner's cinema is one of the victims.[10]

The strategy of remaining inside the circle but on its margins has become increasingly difficult. Tanner has to put a great deal of energy into securing the financial backing for the kind of film he wants to make and even then his films are condemned to limited and inadequate distribution. The result is that Tanner's cinema has become increasingly marginal in relation to the dominant film culture, and the vulnerability of the marginal figure becomes a major concern of the films. In Charles, Paul and Adeline had cut themselves off from all possibility of "a true political engagement," but the characters in the later films find themselves in a completely marginal position as soon as they refuse the social roles expected of them.[11] When Jeanne and Marie take to the road in Messidor, they immediately become outcasts and are placed under tremendous pressures by the social structures from which they are trying to escape; Jonah in the year 2000 in Light Years Away leaves his dead-end job for the dangerous isolation of Yoshka's domain; Paul in In the White City finds himself cast adrift in a foreign city. These marginal characters are pushed outside the circle and their challenge to social norms can then be dismissed as insane or criminal.

Tanner's aim in these films has been "to make the discourse in the images" rather than to develop an ideological discourse as in his earlier films.[12] In keeping with this concern, the characters are less aware of their ideological contexts and are seemingly trapped within their situations. The alternatives seem even more remote than in the earlier films in which they could be conceived, if rarely put into effect. This shrinking of the horizon of the possible clearly reflects political developments since 1968, but the conditional tense is not entirely absent from these films. As Tanner suggests, it is built into the images: while the narrative shows the marginalization and neutralization of characters who refuse to conform, the images evoke "ways of seeing" that suggest the possibility of different perspectives. Despite the absence of explicit ideological concerns in the later films, Tanner still sets up tensions between the codes of realism and a structuralist detachment. The analysis of all of Tanner's films in this study has sought to demonstrate the possibilities of such an approach for a cinema seeking to explore the relationship between personal and political issues. Although these possibilities are currently being obscured by ideological structures that cannot accept such a cinema, Tanner's cinema remains important in the development of a possible challenge to these structures.

NOTES

1. Freddy Buache, "Situation 3," in André Pâquet, ed., Jeune cinéma suisse (Montreal: La Bibliothèque nationale du Québec, 1970), p. 8.

2. Alain Tanner, quoted in Martyn Auty, "A Man Condemned to Stifle Has Escaped," Monthly Film Bulletin, November 1983, p. 316.

3. Yann Lardeau, "Lisbonne, Symphonie d'une ville," Cahiers du cinéma, 346, April 1983, pp. 44.

4. Auty, p. 316.

5. Auty, p. 316.

6. "Alain Tanner: Charles mort ou vif," Cahiers du cinéma, 213, June 1969, p. 28.

7. Michael Tarantino, "Alain Tanner: After Jonah," Sight and Sound, Winter 1978-79, p. 42.

8. "Entretien avec Alain Tanner," Cahiers du cinéma, 273, January-February 1977, p. 40.

9. Tarantino, p. 40.

10. Tanner, "Situation 2," in Pâquet, p. 5.

11. "Tanner: Charles," p. 30.

12. Tanner, quoted in Martyn Auty, "Light Years Away," Monthly Film Bulletin, December 1981, p. 249.

FILMOGRAPHY

In addition to the films listed below, Tanner directed about forty programs for Swiss television (SSR) between 1964 and 1969--including the prize-winning documentary <u>Dr. B., médecin de campagne/Dr. B., Country Doctor</u> (1968). He also collaborated--with Francis Reusser, Anne-Marie Miéville, and Loretta Verna--on a five-week experimental series for the SSR called <u>Ecouter Voir</u> (1977).

NICE TIME (1957)

Directors: Claude Goretta and Alain Tanner. Production: British Film Institute Experimental Production Committee. Photography: John Fletcher. Music: Chas McDevitt Skiffle Group. Sound: John Fletcher. Black and white. 17 minutes.

RAMUZ, PASSAGE D'UN POETE (1961)

Director: Alain Tanner. Production: Actua Films. Screenplay: Franck Jotterand. Photography: Fernand Raymond. Black and white. 27 minutes.

L'ECOLE (1962)

Director: Alain Tanner. Production: Actua Films. Screenplay: Tanner. Photography: Fernand Raymond. Triple screen.

LES APPRENTIS (1964)

Director: Alain Tanner. Production: Teleproduction, Walter Marti. Screenplay: Tanner. Photography: Ernest Artaria. Black and white. 80 minutes.

UNE VILLE A CHANDIGARH (1966)

Director: Alain Tanner. Production: Tanner and Ernest Artaria. Screenplay: Tanner and John Berger. Photography: Artaria. Color. 51 minutes.

CHARLES MORT OU VIF/CHARLES DEAD OR ALIVE (1969)

Director: Alain Tanner. Production: Groupe 5, in collaboration with SSR, Geneva. Screenplay: Tanner. Photography: Renato Berta. Editing: Sylvia Bachmann. Music: Jacques Olivier. Black and white. 90 minutes.
With: François Simon (Charles), Marcel Robert (Paul), Marie-Claire Dufour (Adeline), Maya Simon (Marianne).

LA SALAMANDRE/THE SALAMANDER (1971)

Director: Alain Tanner. Production: Svocine, Geneva. Screenplay: Tanner and John Berger. Photography: Renato Berta. Editing: Brigitte Sousselier. Music: Patrick Moraz. Black and white. 123 minutes.
With: Bulle Ogier (Rosemonde), Jean-Luc Bideau (Pierre), Jacques Denis (Paul).

LE RETOUR D'AFRIQUE/RETURN FROM AFRICA (1973)

Director: Alain Tanner. Production: Groupe 5/SSR (Geneva), Nouvelles Editions de Films/Filmanthrope (Paris). Screenplay: Tanner. Photography: Renato Berta. Editing: Brigitte Sousselier. Music: J. S. Bach, orchestrated by Arie Dzierlatka. Black and white. 104 minutes.
With: Josée Destoop (Françoise), François Marthouret (Vincent), Roger Ibanez (Emilio), Roger Jendly (Marcel), Juliet Berto, Anne Wiazemsky (post office workers).

LE MILIEU DU MONDE/THE MIDDLE OF THE WORLD (1974)

Director: Alain Tanner. Production: Citel Films and SSR (Geneva). Screenplay: Tanner and John Berger. Photography: Renato Berta. Editing: Brigitte Sousselier. Music: Patrick Moraz. Color. 112 minutes.
With: Olimpia Carlisi (Adriana), Philippe Leotard (Paul), Juliet Berto (Juliette), Denise Perron (Mrs Schmidt), Jacques Denis (Marcel), Roger Jendly (Roger).

JONAS QUI AURA 25 ANS EN L'AN 2000/JONAH WHO WILL BE 25 IN THE YEAR 2000 (1976)

Director: Alain Tanner. Production: Citel Films and SSR (Geneva)/Action Films and Société Française de Production (Paris). Screenplay: Tanner and John Berger. Photography: Renato Berta. Editing: Brigitte Sousselier. Music: Jean-Marie Senia. Color. 110 minutes.
With: Jean-Luc Bideau (Max), Myriam Boyer (Mathilde), Jacques Denis (Marco), Roger Jendly (Marcel), Dominique Labourier (Marguerite), Myriam Mézières (Madeleine), Miou-Miou (Marie), Rufus (Mathieu), Raymond Bussières (Charles).

MESSIDOR (1979)

Director: Alain Tanner. Production: Citel Films (Geneva)/ Action Films and Gaumont (Paris). Screenplay: Tanner. Photography: Renato Berta. Editing: Brigitte Sousselier. Music: Arie Dzierlatka. Color. 120 minutes.
With: Clementine Amouroux (Jeanne), Catherine Rétoré (Marie).

LIGHT YEARS AWAY (1981)

Director: Alain Tanner. Production: L.P.A., Phenix, and Slotint (Paris)/SSR (Geneva). Screenplay: Tanner, based on the novel La Voie sauvage by Daniel Odier. Photography: Jean François Robin. Editing: Brigitte Sousselier. Music: Arie Dzierlatka. Color. 105 minutes.
With: Trevor Howard (Yoshka), Mick Ford (Jonah), Bernice Stegers (Betty), Odile Schmitt (the dancer), Joe Pilkinton (Thomas).

DANS LA VILLE BLANCHE/IN THE WHITE CITY   (1983)

Director: Alain Tanner. Production: Filmograph (Geneva)/ Metro Filme (Lisbon). Screenplay: Tanner. Photography: Acacio de Almeida. Editing: Laurent Uhler. Music: Jean-Luc Barbier. Color.
With: Bruno Ganz (Paul), Tereza Madruga, Julia Vonderlinn, José Carvalho, Francisco Baiao.

BIBLIOGRAPHY

SCREENPLAYS

Charles mort ou vif, in L'Avant-scène du cinéma, 108, November 1970.

La Salamandre, in L'Avant-scène du cinéma, 125, May 1972.

Le Milieu du Monde, ou le cinéma selon Tanner, ed. M. Boujut. Lausanne: Editions L'Age d'homme, 1974.

Jonah Who Will Be 25 in the Year 2000, trans. Michael Palmer. Berkeley: North Atlantic Books, 1983.

Jonah Who Will Be 25 in the Year 2000 (extract), Ciné-Tracts, 3, Fall-Winter 1977-78, pp. 7-14.

Les Années lumière (Light Years Away), in L'Avant-scène du cinéma, 270, June 1981.

INTERVIEWS

"Alain Tanner: Charles mort ou vif." Cahiers du cinéma, 213, June 1969, pp. 26-30.

Appignanesi, Richard. "The Screenwriter as Collaborator: An Interview with John Berger." Cineaste, vol. 10, no. 3, Summer 1980, pp. 14-19.

Defrance, Philippe. "Entretien avec Alain Tanner." L'Avant-scène du cinéma, 270, June 1981, pp. 5-7.

"Entretien avec Alain Tanner." Cahiers du cinéma, 273, January-February 1977, pp. 38-43.

Forbes, Jill. "Interview with Alain Tanner." Films and Filming, February 1982, pp. 20-22.

Laurendeau, Francine. "Jean-Luc Bideau, comédien suisse." Cinéma Québec, vol. 3, no. 4, December-January 1973-4, pp. 42-44.

Rubenstein, Lenny. "Alain Tanner: Isolation and Ennui." Film, July 1975, pp. 16-18.

——. "Keeping Hope for Radical Change Alive: An Interview with Alain Tanner." Cineaste, vol. 7, no. 4, Winter 1976-7, pp. 24-25.

Tarantino, Michael. "Alain Tanner: After Jonah." Sight and Sound, Winter 1978-9, pp. 40-43.

ARTICLES AND REVIEWS

Auty, Martyn. "Light Years Away." Monthly Film Bulletin, December 1981, pp. 249-50.

——. "A Man Condemned to Stifle Has Escaped." Monthly Film Bulletin, November 1983, p. 316.

Barron, Fred. "Letter from Switzerland." Take One, vol. 4, no. 11, May-June 1974, pp. 36-37.

Berger, John. "On 'Middle of the Earth'." Ciné-Tracts, 1, Spring 1977, pp. 15-26.

Bucher, Felix. "Charles mort ou vif." International Film Guide, 1970, p. 220.

Callenbach, Ernest. "The Salamander." Film Quarterly, Winter 1972-3, pp. 19-20.

Cargin, Peter. "Charles mort ou vif." Film, Winter 1970, p. 28.

Comolli, Jean-Luc, and Jean Narboni. "Cinema/Ideology/Criticism," in Bill Nicholls, ed., Movies and Methods: An Anthology. Berkeley: University of California Press, 1976, pp. 22-30.

Daney, Serge. "Les huit Ma." Cahiers du cinéma, 273, January-February 1977, pp. 48-50.

Dawson, Jan. "Festivals '73: Berlin." Sight and Sound, Autumn 1973, pp. 225-7.

Debray, Regis. "A Modest Contribution to the Rites and Ceremonies of the Tenth Anniversary." New Left Review, 115, May-June 1979, pp. 45-65.

Durgnat, Raymond. "The Great British Phantasmagoria." Film Comment, May-June 1977, pp. 48-53.

Elia, Maurice. "Jonas qui aura 25 ans en l'an 2000." Séquences, 89, July 1977, pp. 39-41.

Elley, Derek. "La Salamandre." Films and Filming, June 1973, pp. 50-51.

———. "Le Retour d'Afrique." Films and Filming, September 1975, p. 41.

———. "Messidor." Films and Filming, April 1980, pp. 32-33.

Elsaesser, Thomas. "The Cinema of Irony." Monogram, 5, (1973), pp. 1-2.

"The Estates General of the French Cinema, May 1968." Screen, Winter 1972-3, pp. 55-88.

Euvrard, Michel. "Vif à mort." Cinéma Québec, vol. 1, no. 9, May-June 1972, pp. 37-38.

———. "La Salamandre." Cinéma Québec, vol. 1, no. 10, July-August 1972, pp. 36-37.

Fekete, John. "Culture, History and Ambivalence: On the Subject of Walter Benjamin." Ciné-Tracts, 3, Fall-Winter 1977, pp. 30-40.

Gilliatt, Penelope. "Swiss Pride and Prejudice." in Three-Quarter Face: Reports and Reflections. New York: Coward, McCann and Geoghegan, 1980, pp. 227-31.

Gitlin, Todd. "Jonah Who Will Be 25 in the Year 2000."
Film Quarterly, Spring 1977, pp. 36-42.

Greene, Linda, John Hess and Robin Lakes. "Subversive
Charm Indeed!" Jump Cut, 15, (July 1977), pp. 8-9.

Haudiquet, Philippe. "Un enfant du mois de mai." L'Avant-
scène du cinéma, 108, November 1970, pp. 8-9.

Horton, Andrew. "Alain Tanner's Jonah...: Echoes of
Renoir's M. Lange." Film Criticism, vol. IV, no. 3,
Spring 1980, pp. 25-30.

Jacobs, Diane. "The Middle of the World." Take One,
vol. 4, no. 8, November-December 1973, pp. 28-29.

Jaehne, Karen. "Messidor." Film Quarterly, Winter 1979-
80, pp. 53-56.

Kaufmann, Stanley. "La Salamandre; Charles, Dead or
Alive," in Living Images. New York: Harper and Row,
1975, pp. 118-21.

Kazis, Richard, and John Hess. "Jonah Discussed." Jump
Cut, 18, (August 1978), pp. 35-36.

Lardeau, Yann. "Lisbonne, Symphonie d'une ville." Cahiers
du cinéma, 346, April 1983, pp. 44-45.

Lellis, George. "Retreat from Romanticism: Two Films from
the Seventies." Film Quarterly, Summer 1975, pp. 16-
20.

Le Peron, Serge. "Ici ou ailleurs." Cahiers du cinéma,
273, January-February 1977, pp. 44-47.

Lesage, Julia. "Godard and Gorin's Left Politics, 1967-72."
Jump Cut, 28, (April 1983), pp. 51-58.

Martineau, Richard. "Les Années lumière." Séquences,
107, January 1982, pp. 37-39.

Mercken-Spaas, Godelieve. "Narrative Levels in Alain Tanner's La Salamandre." Film Studies Annual, 1977, Part
One, pp. 92-99.

Millar, Gavin. "Messidor." The Listener, 28 February 1980, pp. 278-9.

Monaco, James. "The Costa-Gavras Syndrome." Cineaste, vol. 7, no. 2, Spring 1976, pp. 18-21, 51.

―――. "Swiss Cinema," in Richard Roud, ed., Cinema: A Critical Dictionary. London: Secker and Warburg, 1980, vol. 2, pp. 996-1000.

Pulleine, Tim. "Jonah Who Will Be 25 in the Year 2000." Sight and Sound, Spring 1978, pp. 122-3.

―――. "Messidor." Sight and Sound, Spring 1980, pp. 125-6.

―――. "Tanner's White City." Sight and Sound, Winter 1983-4, p. 5.

Radin, Victoria. "The Salamander." Sight and Sound, Spring 1973, pp. 113-4.

Robbe-Grillet, Alain. "Order and Disorder in Film and Fiction." Critical Inquiry, vol. 4, no. 1, Autumn 1977, pp. 1-20.

Roud, Richard. "The French Line." Sight and Sound, Autumn 1960, pp. 166-71.

Stam, Robert. "The Subversive Charm of Alain Tanner." Jump Cut, 15, (July 1977), pp. 1, 5-7.

Stein, Elliott. "Hit-and-Myth." Film Comment, November-December 1976, pp. 35, 38-9.

Straram, Patrick. "Jonas: Dire le jouir." Cinéma Québec, 50, (1977), pp. 35-36.

Szanto, George. "Oppositional Way-Signs: Some Passages Within John Berger's History-Making, History-Unravelling Experiment." College English, vol. 40, no. 4, December 1978, pp. 364-78.

Tarantino, Michael. "Alain Tanner's Jonah Who Will Be 25 in the Year 2000." Take One, vol. 5, no. 8, March 1977, pp. 13-14.

_____. "Tanner and Berger: The Voice Off-Screen."
Film Quarterly, Winter 1979-80, pp. 32-43.

Thiher, Allen. "The Existential Play in Truffaut's Early
Films." Literature/Film Quarterly, Summer 1977, pp.
183-97.

Toubiana, Serge. "Messidor." Cahiers du cinéma, 299,
April 1979, pp. 47-49.

Weiner, Bernard. "The Long Way Home." Jump Cut, 4,
November-December 1974, pp. 3-4.

Wilson, David. "Festivals '76: Locarno." Sight and
Sound, Autumn 1976, p. 240.

Wu, Ying Wing. "The Long Road to Liberation." Jump
Cut, 7, May-July 1975, pp. 7-8.

BOOKS

Althusser, Louis. Lenin and Philosophy and Other Essays.
Trans. Ben Brewster. London: New Left Books, 1971.

Andrew, J. Dudley. The Major Film Theories: An Introduction. London: Oxford University Press, 1976.

Barthes, Roland. Critical Essays. Trans. Richard Howard.
Evanston: Northwestern University Press, 1972.

Benjamin, Walter. Illuminations. Trans. Harry Zohn. New
York: Harcourt Brace and World, 1968.

Berger, John. About Looking. New York: Pantheon
Books, 1980.

_____. The Moment of Cubism and Other Essays. New
York: Pantheon Books, 1969.

_____. Pig Earth. London: Writers and Readers, 1979.

_____. The Success and Failure of Picasso. New York:
Pantheon Books, 1980.

_____. Ways of Seeing. Harmondsworth: Penguin, 1972.

_____ and Jean Mohr. A Fortunate Man: The Story of a Country Doctor. London: Writers and Readers, 1976.

_____. A Seventh Man: Migrant Workers in Europe. New York: Viking Press, 1975.

Bloch, Ernst, Georg Lukacs, Bertolt Brecht, Walter Benjamin, Theodor Adorno. Aesthetics and Politics. London: New Left Books, 1977.

Césaire, Aimé. Return to My Native Land. Trans. John Berger and Anna Bostock. Harmondsworth: Penguin, 1969.

Chatman, Seymour, Umberto Eco, Jean-Marie Klinkenberg (eds.). A Semiotic Landscape/Panorama sémiotique. The Hague: Mouton, 1979.

Cohn-Bendit, Gabriel, and Daniel Cohn-Bendit. Obsolete Communism: The Left-Wing Alternative. Trans. Arnold Pomerans. Harmondsworth: Penguin, 1969.

Debord, Guy. Society of the Spectacle. Detroit: Black and Red, 1970.

Demetz, Peter (ed.). Brecht: A Collection of Critical Essays. Englewood Cliffs, N.J.: Prentice-Hall, 1962.

Eidsvik, Charles. Cineliteracy: Film Among the Arts. New York: Random House, 1978.

Foucault, Michel. The History of Sexuality. Vol. 1: An Introduction. Trans. Robert Hurley. New York: Vintage Books, 1980.

Gelmis, Joseph (ed.). The Film Director as Superstar. New York: Doubleday, 1970.

Goodman, Paul. Utopian Essays and Practical Proposals. New York: Random House, n.d.

Graham, Peter (ed.). The New Wave: Critical Landmarks. London: Secker and Warburg, 1968.

Harvey, Sylvia. May '68 and Film Culture. London: British Film Institute, 1978.

Haskell, Molly. From Reverence to Rape: The Treatment of Women in the Movies. New York: Holt, Rinehart and Winston, 1974.

Jameson, Fredric. The Prison-House of Language: A Critical Account of Structuralism and Russian Formalism. Princeton: Princeton University Press, 1972.

Lefebvre, Henri. Everyday Life in the Modern World. Trans. Sacha Rabinovitch. London: Allen Lane, 1971.

_____. L'idéologie structuraliste. Paris: Editions Anthropos, 1971.

Lellis, George. Bertolt Brecht, Cahiers du Cinéma and Contemporary Film Theory. Ann Arbor, Michigan: UMI Research Press, 1982.

Lévi-Strauss, Claude. Tristes Tropiques. Trans. John and Doreen Weightman. New York: Atheneum, 1974.

Lovell, Alan, and Jim Hillier. Studies in Documentary. London: Secker and Warburg, 1972.

Maclaglan, David. Creation Myths: Man's Introduction to the World. London: Thames and Hudson, 1977.

Marcorelles, Louis. Living Cinema: New Directions in Contemporary Film-making. Trans. Isabel Quigly. New York: Praeger Publishers, 1973.

Milne, Tom (ed.). Godard on Godard. London: Secker and Warburg, 1972.

Pâquet, André (ed.). Jeune cinéma suisse. Montreal: La Bibliothèque nationale du Québec, 1970.

Paz, Octavio. Alternating Current. Trans. Helen R. Lane. New York: Viking Press, 1973.

_____. The Bow and the Lyre. Trans. Ruth L.C. Simms. Austin: University of Texas Press, 1973.

―――――. Conjunctions and Disjunctions. Trans. Helen R. Lane. New York: Viking Press, 1974.

Posner, Charles (ed.). Reflections on the Revolution in France: 1968. Harmondsworth: Penguin, 1970.

Robbe-Grillet, Alain. For a New Novel: Essays on Fiction. Trans. Richard Howard. New York: Grove Press, 1965.

Rousseau, Jean-Jacques. Emile: Or, On Education. Trans. Allan Bloom. New York: Basic Books, 1979.

Scheede, Uwe M. René Magritte: Life and Work. Trans. W. Walter Jaffe. Woodbury, N.Y.: Barron's, 1982.

Simon, John K. (ed.). Modern French Criticism: From Proust and Valéry to Structuralism. Chicago: University of Chicago Press, 1972.

Singer, Daniel. Prelude to Revolution: France in May 1968. New York: Hill and Wang, 1970.

Sussex, Elizabeth. Lindsay Anderson. London: Studio Vista, 1969.

Thompson, E. P. The Poverty of Theory and Other Essays. New York: Monthly Review Press, 1978.

Williams, Raymond. Keywords: A Vocabulary of Culture and Society. Glasgow: Fontana, 1976.

―――――. The Long Revolution. London: Chatto and Windus, 1961.

―――――. Politics and Letters: Interviews with New Left Review. London: New Left Books, 1979.

INDEX

Letters in brackets indicate locations of photos in illustration section.

Adorno, Theodor 34
Althusser, Louis 29-30, 33
Anderson, Lindsay 8, 11, 13; Everyday Except Christmas, 9, 11; O Dreamland, 8; This Sporting Life, 10

Barthes, Roland 38-39
Bazin, André 13-15, 27-28, 42, 138, 152
Beckett, Samuel Waiting For Godot, 8
Benayoun, Robert 15
Benjamin, Walter 66, 141, 149n
Berger, John 6, 12, 16, 33-40, 44, 46, 55, 90, 106, 109, 113, 117-20, 122-23, 125, 151-52; A Fortunate Man, 36; A Painter of Our Time, 37; Pig Earth, 152; A Seventh Man, 37
Brecht, Bertolt 8, 15, 28, 30, 32, 40-42, 45, 47-48, 57, 138
Buache, Freddy 5, 180

Cahiers du cinéma 13, 15, 19-20
Cesaire, Aimé Return to My Native Land, 36, 90-91, 95-96, 103-04
Chabrol, Claude 13; Le Beau Serge, 13
Char, René 69
Cornand, André 57
Costa-Gavras, Constantin Z, 21
cubism 38-39

Daney, Serge 127, 136, 138, 147
Debord, Guy 45
DeFrance, Philippe 178
Dziga Vertov collective, The 20; British Sounds, 21

Eisenstein, Sergei 28
Elley, Derek 98
Elsaesser, Thomas 87
Ernst, Max 34
Estates General of the French Cinema, The 19
Euvrard, Michel 84

Fassbinder, Rainer Werner 4
Filmcollectif Zurich, Cinema Dead or Alive 23n

Foucault, Michel 71
Free Cinema 3, 7-14, 22, 27, 48, 76

Garvey, Marcus 95
Gitlin, Todd 33, 44-46, 119, 144
Godard, Jean-Luc 14-15, 28, 30-31, 103, 104-05n; Breathless, 14; La Chinoise, 17, 20; Le Gai Savoir, 20: Tout va bien, 20-21; Weekend, 20, 91
Goretta, Claude 1, 8; The Lacemaker, 3, 5; The Madman, 3
Gorin, Jean-Pierre 20
Gozlan, Gérard 14-15
Grierson, John 9
Groupe Cinq 3

Haudiquet, Philippe 58-59
Heine, Heinrich 75-76

Jacobs, Diane 107, 114, 119-20
Jaehne, Karen 155, 160, 162
Jalée, Pierre 93
Jameson, Fredric 42
Jennings, Humphrey 9
Jump Cut 31, 132, 146-47

Lefebvre, Henri 29, 33-34, 46, 65, 68-69, 82
Le Peron, Serge 6, 34, 45, 60
Lévi-Strauss, Claude 143

Magritte, René 34-35
Marcorelles, Louis 2, 9, 47
Martineau, Richard 175
Marx, Karl 19, 29, 36, 143-44, 147
May 1968 7, 16-22, 27-29, 31, 33, 35, 58, 126, 128, 132, 144, 151, 160, 182
Mercken-Spaas, Godelieve 87
Millar, Gavin 152, 158
Moraz, Patricia The Indians Are Still Far Away, 88n
Moullet, Luc 14

neorealism 14
New Left, The 7-8, 11-12, 28, 30, 32
New Wave, The 7, 12-17, 21-22, 27

Osborne, John Look Back in Anger, 7-8, 12
Ozu, Yasujiro 119

Pasolini, Pier Paolo 103; Theorem, 104-05n
Paz, Octavio 27-29, 41, 46-47, 141, 143, 149n
Piaget, Jean 130
Positif 14-15, 27

Pulleine, Tim 152

realism 15, 22, 27-28, 32-35, 39, 42-47, 119, 144, 147, 152, 168, 175, 183
Reed, Carol The Third Man, 2
Reisz, Karel Saturday Night and Sunday Morning, 10; We Are the Lambeth Boys, 9-10
Renard, Jules 68
Richardson, Tony Look Back in Anger, 10, 23n
Robbe-Grillet, Alain 71
Rossi-Landi, Ferruccio 47
Roud, Richard 13, 15
Rousseau, Jean-Jacques 38, 126-28, 130, 135, 139-41, 147

Said, Edward L. 30
Schmid, Daniel 4
Sequence 13
Sight and Sound 13
Soutter, Michel 1, 4; The Escapade, 3; The Surveyors, 3
Stam, Robert 33, 42-43, 48, 129, 147
structuralism 22, 28-30, 32-33, 35, 38-40, 42, 46-47, 119-20, 130, 144, 172, 183
surrealism 34-35
Sussex, Elizabeth 9
Switzerland 1-7, 31, 59, 62, 72-3, 83-85, 144, 151, 167, 180-82
Syberberg, Hans-Jürgen 4
Szanto, George 37, 39-40

Tanner, Alain Charles Dead or Alive, 1, 3-6, 16, 29, 31, 34, 36, 43, 47, 49, 55-69, 71, 75-76, 82, 84, 92, 94, 97, 100, 106, 113, 122, 133-34, 139, 153-55, 158, 170-71, 178, 181-82, [A]; A City at Chandigarh, 35-36; Dr. B., Country Doctor, 3, 36, 58; In the White City, 180-82, [L]; Jonah Who Will Be 25 in the Year 2000, 3, 5, 31, 33-34, 36, 41-42, 46, 48, 125-48, 152, 159, 169-70, 173-74, 176, 178, 182, [F-H]; Light Years Away, 5, 167-78, 182-82, [K]; Messidor, 3, 5-6, 48-49, 151-65, 167, 169-70, 172, 177-78, 180-82, [I-J]; The Middle of the World, 16, 29, 34, 48, 74, 106-23, 128, 132, 139, 146, 148n, 157, 172, 176, 178, 181, [D-F]; Nice Time, 8; Return from Africa, 29, 34, 36-37, 43, 48, 73, 90-104, 106, 108, 113, 123, 125, 128, 132-33, 152, 168, 173, 180, [C-D]; The Salamander, 29, 34-35, 48, 71-88, 100, 106, 108, 128, 132, 138, 152, 160, 163, 169, 173-74, 176-78, [B-C]
Tarantino, Michael 39-40, 76-77
Thompson, E.P. 30
Toubiana, Serge 167
Truffaut, François Les Mistons, 13

Velan, Yves 29

Weiner, Bernard 102
Williams, Raymond 11-12, 32-33, 41-42, 46, 55, 58, 90
Wu, Ying Wing 107-78, 119

OHIO UNIVERSITY LIBRARY

Please return this book as soon as you have finished with it. In order to avoid a fine it must be returned by the latest date stamped below. All books are subject to recall after two weeks or immediately if needed for reserve.

CF